# SpringerBriefs in Political Science

More information about this series at http://www.springer.com/series/8871

Max Meyer

# Liberal Democracy

## Prosperity through Freedom

 Springer

Max Meyer
Bern, Switzerland

ISSN 2191-5466          ISSN 2191-5474   (electronic)
SpringerBriefs in Political Science
ISBN 978-3-030-47407-2      ISBN 978-3-030-47408-9   (eBook)
https://doi.org/10.1007/978-3-030-47408-9

This book is an open access publication.

This Springer imprint is published by the registered company Springer Nature Switzerland AG.
The registered company address is: Gewerbestrasse 11, 6330 Cham, Switzerland

# Preface

Never before in the history of mankind have people fared so well. For the first time, many of us are experiencing longer periods of time free from epidemics, famine, and war at home. There is an astonishing level of prosperity throughout vast areas of the globe—not only for the wealthier classes but for many others as well. But where are these privileged societies going? Do they have any kind of long-term goal—any particular mission? And if they do, do they know how they want to get there? Or are they leaving things up to fate as they go about their daily business?

Why do some countries prosper while others fail? What determines the success of a country or for that matter a company? Why do some countries or companies stagnate?

In this book, I will address these questions. First, I will look at how European culture differs from other cultures and consider the importance of human rights in relation to prosperity and well-being. I will then discuss liberalism, its strengths and weaknesses, and the conditions necessary for economic success, one of the most important being a stable democracy—a liberal democracy. Finally, I will formulate various theses intended as a guide to help politicians, decision-makers, and young people shape a successful future.

Prosperity is not a law of nature; it must be worked for. Freedom, democracy, a functioning state, and a strong middle class create the necessary foundation for prosperity and provide the basis for its sustainability. In this book, I would like to show which factors are decisive for a society to rise to the top and what drives or hinders people as they strive for meaningful, value-creating activities and happiness. Living in a welfare state can easily distract citizens from this focus. Political parties and ideologues continue to provoke society with old and even new approaches that simply do not work.

As a Swiss citizen, I do not intend to criticize other countries or even the European Union, but merely to analyze them. I know that I am presenting an outsider's point of view, which the reader may or may not accept. It is my hope that now as I stand at the end of my professional career, I can pass on the experience and knowledge I have gained as a lawyer, as a founder and owner of various companies, as a member of the board of directors of larger companies, as an investor, and also, to a limited extent, as a politician.

This book is not based solely on my own original thoughts. Many other authors have also written about the subjects presented here. This book is the result of my reflections on these issues. After all, perspective is individual, and the importance of any topic is subject to the author's own perceptions.

I would like to thank Robert Lombardini, my friend from a summer spent together at Stanford University in 1991, and also my friend Peter Everts for his constructive criticism of the text and his suggestions for the content.

Bern, Switzerland                                                              Max Meyer

# Contents

# Chapter 1
# European Values

## 1.1 Value Systems

How do we humans perceive the world and what distinguishes us from animals?

Animals live in the moment, the concrete present. They are aware of themselves. A dog knows who it is, knows its own name and reacts to it. But it has no extended consciousness; it cannot imagine things and therefore, unlike humans, it is not capable of including the past and its expectations for the future in its evaluation of the present.

By contrast, humans can imagine things. They can envision things that do not exist in reality, but only in their imaginations—in their plans, their goals, their aspirations, and their dreams.

*Humans can imagine things that do not exist.*

By including the future or the past in our considerations and, while doing so, imagining things that simply do not exist, we can plan and shape the future.

This ability enables us to build a *set of values*. By creating concepts that are a product of our fantasy, we can establish ways of thinking and behaving that we consider to be correct. Many people develop their own behavioral rules by establishing principles according to which they conduct their lives. Often, however, these ways of thinking and behaving are not shaped by the individual. Rather, they come from the culture into which we are born. From our childhood onward, we perceive them as a set of values to live by. Sometimes we are inspired by a role model, i.e. a leader who propagates a set of values. Others begin to adhere to these rules. The leader can be religious or political. Religious leaders may be cult leaders, gurus, even founders of religions, or prophets. Political leaders who create and spread their own sets of values are autocrats or dictators such as Hitler, who, in fact, introduced National Socialism as a set of values. Such value systems can develop over a long period of time and, as the example of religion shows us, they can also last for a very long time. Yet, they can also emerge and disappear again quite quickly, as we can see in the codes of conduct adopted by youth gangs or sects.

© The Author(s) 2020
M. Meyer, *Liberal Democracy*, SpringerBriefs in Political Science,
https://doi.org/10.1007/978-3-030-47408-9_1

A value system consists of *common ideas* and *common rules of behavior* for a group of people.

Some questions that address the idea and behavioral patterns include: What should we believe in and what is considered heretical? How do we greet each other? By shaking hands, by bowing to each other, by giving the Hitler salute, or as young people do today, by slapping upraised hands? Is premarital sex allowed or strictly forbidden? Is there a positive attitude towards homosexuality (as in ancient Greece) or negative? Is killing other humans allowed and if so, when (in war, in retaliation, or as a death penalty)? Are we in favor of democracy or do we prefer strong central leadership (autocracy or even National Socialism, etc.)?

Unlike animals, humans can create *value systems*. There were and are numerous value systems in which humans live. We call them ideologies, religions or cultures (even a corporate culture is such a system). These value systems connect those concerned (a clan, a company or a whole nation), and hold them together, enabling them to *strive toward a common goal*. And it is because of these systems that humans are capable of building organizations; no animal could build a NASA.

Because the people in a value system share the same views, it is possible to create a feeling of unity within the group—be it a clan or thousands of individuals—and then steer their activities in the same direction. Today it is possible to align and mobilize larger masses of people towards the same shared values. This is how political ideologies, myths, or even religions were created.

By living in a society with other "like-minded people", humans perceive their value system as their culture and therefore as equitable. They will rarely question it seriously. On the contrary, they will defend it with irrational arguments and respond emotionally and at worst aggressively. But if they doubt the value system in which they live, they will rarely say so publicly, because doing so would place them in the minority and they would become outsiders. Accordingly, examining such systems from the outside and determining which system is really fair and which system brings moral or economic progress to humanity is justified. Justifications made by supporters living within a system lack sufficient rationality.


## 1.2 Development of Human Rights


*Human rights* are one of the most important value systems of all and have been gaining enormously in importance all over the world. In the western world they have become the very basis of coexistence.

*Europe is the cradle of human rights.*

Human rights are a European achievement and while they have been adopted in areas with a European heritage (the USA, Canada, Australia, etc.) and in some Asian countries (Japan, South Korea, Taiwan), they still lack tradition in other parts of the world, where they are often rejected. They have developed in steps over the centuries and were often followed by autocratic phases in which freedoms were once again suppressed. Historically, this has happened in cycles. What is important is that human rights did not get lost in this process. Instead, they have remained in human consciousness and taken on even stronger forms. They continue to develop today.

Freedom of opinion and freedom of speech as the core of human rights were already considered to be essential in ancient Greece, where democracy was tested for the first time. They were adopted in Rome during the Republican phase. However, these rights were granted only to Roman citizens who were allowed to express themselves freely during public assemblies. Many others were subjected to inhumane slavery within the society. Human rights were also suppressed during the Middle Ages. In this dark period of European history, the value system was dictated from above by an authoritarian regime. God, as represented by his governors on earth as well as secular rulers, determined how human beings were to behave and what they were to believe.

It was not until the reformation that people once again railed against autocratic authorities. The European Enlightenment then ushered in change reaching an initial zenith during the French Revolution with calls of *Liberté, Egalité, Fraternité* demanding freedom and equality for people. Churches were plundered and secularized. The royal family was beheaded. The freedoms of opinion and speech enjoyed during ancient times were revived. These values were honed and came to include freedom of assembly and freedom of the press. Later, the right to own property and the principle of freedom of trade and industry were added. Of course, each epoch has its roots in previous ones. Even the Enlightenment, which was a time when people came to be considered rational beings who could decide independently about matters of truth and fallacy, had its roots in the philosophies of thinkers from earlier times. There have also been setbacks, for example, during the time of Napoleon, who involved all of Europe in war; or, more recently seen, during the last two horrific world wars.

It is, however, important to note that the desire for freedom and justice that had been awakened in the minds of people stayed with them and it was not possible for an autocrat to completely suppress this desire. On the contrary, after every setback, human rights have taken on improved forms; they were honed and even secured in the European Human Rights Convention. They have been included in the constitutions of most modern European countries as well as in the Universal Declaration of Human Rights of the United Nations, which means that they should actually apply worldwide.

## 1.3  Separation of Church and State

An important step was the separation of church and state, which in Europe meant not only separating the church from the state but requiring the church to submit to the rules of the state. The authoritarian political structure created by the church and the crown during the Middle Ages, which dictated values from above, was gradually replaced. With the church now subordinate to the state, government authorities established a system of values through laws, which were increasingly adopted through democratic processes. Many of these laws were in direct opposition to religious values, reducing the influence of the Church. The more democratically and economically developed a region became, the less influence the church had.

Western Christian tradition is sometimes referred to as a value and is equated with humanism, freedom of expression, and even religious freedom and peace. This view assumes that such values are realized because of the role they play in western *Christian* culture. However, this point of view fails to recognize that the changes brought about by the Reformation and especially the Enlightenment were necessary in order to give individuals back the freedom to think whatever they wanted. Only since then have people been free in their beliefs. Religious freedom is based on western *liberal* tradition. It was enforced against the will of Catholic institutions and the aristocracy. Ultimately, civil liberties are not based in the Christianity of the Roman Catholic Church of the day, but in the subordination and subjugation of the church to governmental laws that respect the tradition of human rights and democracy. In the Middle Ages, Christianity, like many religions, was neither peaceful nor liberal. The Church was intolerant, considered Christianity to be the only true religion, and demanded it be spread though missionary work. It was only because of the Reformation and especially the Enlightenment, as well as the de facto dissolution of the Papal States by Napoleon, that the Church became a peaceful western tradition.

The Roman Catholic Church as an autocratic institution has to be differentiated from a Christianity that could be interpreted differently from the Bible than it is by Catholic hierarchies with their claim of infallibility. Christianity must also be differentiated from the individual faiths that are respected today in most of the forms which humans have developed in their fantasies. These beliefs have nothing in common with an ecclesiastical clerical set of values.

The concept of "God" has changed over time. Because humans can imagine things which do not exist, in antiquity they fabricated a world of gods by telling stories which included gods, ghosts, fairies, etc. Later this concept changed. The earlier myths were replaced by the concept of a God, whereby there were also always other divine beings around (angels, saints, etc.). This God is all powerful. He can be prayed to; He leads His people, and He can perform miracles. However, this concept of God as a mastermind, who can communicate with millions of people individually and who even supports opposing sides[1] in a conflict, also became implausible during the course of the Enlightenment. The concepts of God changed again. In western welfare states in particular, there is a trend away from religion. The number of agnostics, who only believe in a distant power, as well as the number of atheists is increasing.[2] According to the most recent surveys, very few people in Europe still

---

[1] In previous wars, priests on both sides supported the conflict and even blessed the cannons.

[2] There are people who provide proof of God's existence based on visions they have had. They have experienced something that can only be explained by divine intervention. This is difficult to dispute because the more such stories are told, the more realistic the phenomena become. Believing in them is in keeping with our right to freedom of religion. An enlightened humanist thinks that these are hallucinations or perhaps simply boasting and believes what he or she wants. But each individual

believe in either heaven or hell, and only 40% of people believe in life after death.[3] If there is no life after death, is there even a God?

## 1.4 Democracy with Separation of Powers

The absolute entitlement of the monarchy and the authoritarian behavior of the Catholic church have been set aside in the west. Despite numerous setbacks, a value system based on human rights—especially individual freedoms—has emerged since the Enlightenment.

However, so that these values could be guaranteed in the long term, it was also necessary to adapt the authority of the State. Autocratic rulers were no longer tolerated.[4] Montesquieu advocated the separation of powers, which became the system of "checks and balances" in the United States. Democracy could be established. It was based on the power of the people. This new value system created in Europe is *democracy based on human rights.*[5]

---

belief has nothing to do with clerical value systems dictated by church authorities. On the contrary, it is only possible (and does not lead to witch hunts) thanks to the freedom of opinion guaranteed by the state.

[3]Based on a survey commissioned by *Der Spiegel*, a leading German news magazine, in March 2019 (issue 17/2019 from April 4, 2019), 55% of Germans believe in "one God". 40% believe in angels or on life after death; the age group closest to death are especially skeptical: only 29% of those 65 and older believe in life after death. Among the younger people surveyed, the number was well over 40%. 13% still believe in hell and 26% in the devil. According to an INSA survey commissioned by the newspaper, *Bild*, for Whitsunday, 39.2% of Germans believe there is a God. 51.8% do not. 29.3% believe that heaven exists and 14.5% believe in hell.

[4]The last autocratic ruler in Western Europe is the Pope.

[5]In Europe there is no clash of religions (Christians vs. Muslim). Rather there is a clash of systems, namely between the secular system, which makes the church subordinate to state regulations, and the value system dictated by the church. Many immigrants come from unenlightened regions. A great deal of effort is needed to explain the secular system to them.

# Chapter 2
# Liberalism

## 2.1 Liberal Market Economy

Human rights, especially individual freedoms together with other fundamental rights such as the right to own property and the principle of freedom of trade and industry, led to a market economy and to a system known as *capitalism*. However, this word has a negative connotation for some people. In the twentieth century, capitalism stood in opposition to communism. At that time people could only really choose to become either a capitalist or a communist. Because many leftists felt that communism was the only system that could bring justice to the world, they disparaged capitalism to the point that many people still consider capitalists to be wealthy exploiters who humiliate and abuse the poor. Consequently, in this text I will replace the word "capitalism" with "liberalism", which I understand to mean a free market economy in combination with human rights as well as democracy.

Liberalism requires a functioning legal system and an educated citizenry as well as a largely homogeneous value system. A medieval market without legal protection but with the dominance of the powerful was not enough. What is needed is full recognition of civil liberties, legal protection for everyone, protection of property (including intellectual property), etc.—in other words, a state governed by the rule of law.

Liberalism has been successful in many countries and has contributed significantly to the well-being of numerous people. For the *first time* in the several thousand-year-old history of mankind, many are living in freedom because of liberalism. It has also contributed to a dramatic increase in prosperity for many as well as to tremendous technical and scientific progress.

The free market economy in particular forces each competitor to be better than the other. The objective is to further success with innovation and inventiveness. In the meantime, left-leaning systems have failed. There is not a single example of a leftist system that has been successful.

However, the system is only equitable when capital and labor are well balanced.

© The Author(s) 2020
M. Meyer, *Liberal Democracy*, SpringerBriefs in Political Science,
https://doi.org/10.1007/978-3-030-47408-9_2

We know that capitalism can lead to inequality and to the accumulation of wealth and power of a select group. In such situations, universal prosperity is no longer being fostered by the liberal system, but rather the prosperity of a wealthy and powerful elite. For this reason, liberalism needs rules that prevent this and I will address these later. They lay the foundation for democracy. Abuses of power are prevented wherever citizens have the power and when everyone has the same rights and responsibilities as well as access to the same level of transparency and information. If every citizen has a vote, the laws ensure that everyone shares in prosperity.

The system will only lead to sustainable prosperity and to the long-term satisfaction of free citizens[1] when the liberal market economy is linked to a genuine democracy that also includes freedom of the press and freedom of information. We refer to this system as a *liberal democracy*.

## 2.2   Freedom of Opinion Also Extends to Lateral Thinkers

Constant competition within a free market requires that products and services be continually refined and improved. This can only be done by people who are allowed to think and act freely. It requires proactive individuals who see market niches, listen to customers and take risks, and who can turn ideas into reality. These people drive progress. However, they alone are not enough to advance development so that it reaches that last small but decisive quantum level. This requires creative *lateral thinkers*—mavericks who go beyond conventional limits to formulate their opinions and develop new ideas. These lateral thinkers are not always pleasant because they question everything and rattle existing power structures. Nor are they always right or successful. Many of their ideas will fail because they are unrealistic or downright wrong. Only a few of them will lead to breakthroughs. A free system has to tolerate such mavericks, and nothing should be allowed to happen to them. They can only be active in a liberal system. They must have freedom of thought and freedom of speech. This is true not only for the innovation of products and services but also for the political system in general. Society is also changing and developing. And here too, lateral thinkers have contributed successfully to new developments.

While very courageous dissidents have only occasionally confronted repressive autocratic political systems and risked their lives for their values, liberal progress with its freedom of opinion and freedom of speech has led to many extreme lateral thinkers, who have consequently driven political and economic innovation.

---

[1]The system reaches its limits in areas where billionaires use the most modern advertising methods to influence less well-educated citizens so that the poor unknowingly vote for the interests of the rich (the Tea Party and other movements in the USA). Democracy can only be built on education. (Refer to Chap. 9).

## 2.3 Progress Without Freedom?

There are countries that would like to benefit from the market economy and participate in economic growth without respecting human rights. They argue that they have a different culture which must be respected. European human rights do not belong to their culture.

These countries (such as China, Russia, or those with a theocratic/religious system as in many Middle Eastern countries) claim that their values take precedence over human rights. These values are enforced by a centralized authority and, if necessary, in a manner which is antithetical to human rights. Under the pretext of protecting their countries from outside interference, the leaders of these countries claim that their cultures must be safeguarded from European values. Human rights can then be rejected because they are classified as European values. They ignore the fact that the concept of individual freedom, which accepts lateral thinkers, is a prerequisite for progress to grow in new directions. Using a centralized government to protect the existing culture and political structures prevents the final decisive steps of innovation. Restricting human rights because of such values prevents the final phases of progress. Countries or regimes that protect their own cultural values from human rights will never make it to the top. This applies to all centrally or autocratically governed countries without political change.

To achieve the possible, you have to continually try the impossible.[2]

In addition, once awakened, individual civil liberties become a fundamental need of every human being. In this respect all people are the same. Such needs cannot be denied by suggesting they belong to another culture, other circumstances, or different values. A look at present-day Europe and its surroundings shows that within the core of Europe there are now stable democracies. These countries are unlikely to go to war with each other, as they did during two world wars. Conflicts have shifted to the periphery of Europe. In all of these conflicts—whether in the Ukraine, the Middle Eastern countries or in former Yugoslavia—many people long for the European values of freedom and democracy, while the ruling castes continue to try and defend their privileges. In the long run, they will not be able to maintain their hold and European values will even undermine the Russian regime, because wherever there is freedom, people look toward it and emigrate to those places. This is also true in Asia as can be seen in Hong Kong, where over a million people have participated in mass protests (July 2019); or in South America where mass protests are taking place in many different countries. If people have known freedom, they reject restrictions such as the extradition of their citizens to countries which do not have independent courts. They value freedom more than economic prosperity; they feel more at ease in a society without autocratic despotism and willingly accept economic hardship in return—all the more so as worldwide communication reveals that the liberal system is ultimately more successful. China and Russia will also have to learn this.

---

[2]Hermann Hesse (1877–1962).

## 2.4    From Prosperity to Well-Being

In developing countries, development progresses from *prosperity* to *well-being*.

Starving people and those who have nothing strive for *prosperity*. They can see that other regions on the planet are doing well and they want their countries to follow suit. They want a standard of living that allows them to have not only enough to eat, but also some extras that go beyond basic survival—such as holidays, a car, a good education for their children, medical care, etc. In order to have this, they will accept dictatorial leadership, as long as it pursues this goal credibly. Such leadership is often more goal-oriented than that in a democracy. Things move forward more quickly. In addition, these people are often used to such a hierarchical order even if the state disregards human rights when pursuing these goals. However, this type of leadership will only be accepted under the condition that it strives for the good of all and makes use of competent economic experts. If autocrats are only concerned with their own power, which is usually the case, the emphasis on successful liberalism or progress via technocrats does not appear to be credible.

Once a country has achieved a certain level of prosperity, people also begin to wish for a sense of *well-being*. This includes a desire for freedom (freedom of opinion, freedom of speech, freedom of assembly, and freedom of the press) as well as the rule of law (independent courts, no corruption, etc.). In concrete terms, people want to have the freedom to criticize their government without fear of going to prison. They want to have the freedom to file a lawsuit against the state or the freedom to travel wherever they want. For it is only in such an environment that people really feel at ease. And it is only such a free society that creates the climate necessary to catch up with other similarly free societies and participate at the leading edge of research and development.

A free society is based on democracy—a democracy with a stable constitution and laws, as well as independent courts, so that there is no threat of being picked up in the middle of the night and forced into silence. It is based on a culture that insists on free elections, on human rights, and human dignity. This culture must be so stable that freedom and the rule of law have become sacrosanct.[3] Although not all democracies are equally successful, it is only within democracies that the freedoms of humans are protected. *There is not a single political system in the world which protects human rights that is not also a democracy.*

South Korea, Taiwan, Singapore and other countries rose to prosperity with dictatorial leadership and then made the transition to democracy and the rule of law (in South Korea a former dictatorial president was given a prison sentence by the

---

[3]In his book *The Future is Asian*, Parag Khanna uses the example of Asian nations to repeatedly emphasize that autocratic leadership by technocrats is more efficient than a democracy because it more effectively pursues the goal of economic success. However, such leadership limits the goal to economic progress; assumes that leadership acts in the interest of everyone and not only in the interest of its own power; and it neglects the fact that people educated for progress only really feel comfortable living in freedom and in a constitutional state with democratic participation.

courts for corruption). Meanwhile, the numerous demonstrations by young people in economically rising areas (Hong Kong, Moscow, Kiev, Istanbul, various South American countries, etc.) show that there will ultimately be a demand for a transition from prosperity to a sense of well-being. China, too, will have to abandon its police state if it wishes to take the final step toward becoming a leading nation.

The West and other freedom-loving nations will prevail as long as they continue to defend human rights within a resolute democratic system and other nations fail to do so.

Europe brought the world the system of human rights linked with a market economy. Human rights are the most important contribution Europe has made to the world.

# Chapter 3
# Change and Its Consequences

## 3.1 Change and the Consequences of Liberalism

Liberalism demands accelerated change and requires that people respond to this change.

Freedom of opinion and expression enabled people to break away from rigid medieval dogmas and pursue new ideas without fear of repercussion. Now all scientific directions could be developed without prejudice. Not only did the humanities advance into new areas, there were also countless technical innovations and inventions. The world of the middle-ages underwent change at an increasingly accelerated pace—a pace that has continued to pick up exponentially to this day.

While new discoveries were left to chance in earlier times, research has now been systemized like never before. Both universities and companies invest in research and development and therefore in change. Thanks to worldwide communication, the results are usually accessible to everyone and researchers can integrate their findings with those of others around the globe. As a result, the intervals between innovations have become shorter and shorter. In all scientific areas, the pace of progress is advancing faster than ever before.

Not only is the world of technology changing, the personal circumstances in which we live are changing as well. In the past, very few people relocated. It was normal to live and die where they had been born. Today, just the opposite is true. The psychological hurdle of picking up roots and leaving home is much lower and people have become more flexible. The same is true for relationships. We change our friends, business partners and jobs regularly whereas in the past, these usually lasted a lifetime. Even marriage, considered sacred in the Middle Ages with vows of faithfulness until death, often ends in divorce today. As a result, with longer life expectancy, many people will experience a series of longer relationships during their lifetime. "Serial marriage" has become a reality.

Rapid change has become the norm in organizations (companies, administration, the state) as well. Technology, work processes, products, market, demand or needs,

M. Meyer, *Liberal Democracy*, SpringerBriefs in Political Science,
https://doi.org/10.1007/978-3-030-47408-9_3

and sales methods are all changing. New insights into the optimization of human interaction has led to new management structures. New products and services lead to new companies while old ones disappear. The result is continuous economic and social change.

## 3.2   The Consequences of Change

In addition to change, modern humans are exposed to other impressions and stimuli. Outside of their homes, they no longer move about in nature, but must be aware of other stressed commuters. People are bombarded by news delivered via modern communication methods such as cell phones, tablets and television.

Constant change and exposure to stimuli force people to react defensively. Modern humans filter out images and experiences that are not important to them. They experience these things superficially, even if they are powerful experiences. On the other hand, this flood of stimuli has strengthened modern humans' mental capacity. Their sensitivity threshold is much higher than before. In the past, humans, who were normally exposed to fewer stimuli than today were easily overwhelmed and left perplexed by situations which created a flood of sensations. By contrast, young people today, who constantly use their smartphones or headphones, give the impression that they need a certain number of stimuli to calm their minds.

## 3.3   Obstructers

There are, nevertheless, people who only feel comfortable in the region where their families have always lived and with their well-established ways of life. They become frightened by rapid change so they resist it, perceiving it as a threat that they must fight. Their behavior means that change comes about in the face of opposition—in other words, slowly. Apparently, the better off people are, the more lethargic and less interested in change they become. During periods of economic boom, the number of people who are satisfied with their lives increases. These people resist change, preferring to rest on what they have achieved. This slows the speed of change. If, however, the standard of living decreases, the fighting spirit is revived by those who want to regain competitiveness, i.e. those who want to promote change through renewal. Consequently, progress comes in cycles. The willingness to accept change decreases during economic booms. This leads to stagnation and recession. During lean periods, people work harder; they catch up with structural changes; and growth increases, creating a new boom phase.

This system also has its casualties. They are the price paid for rapid progress. It is therefore important to have a social safety net. The faster the speed of change, the larger the number of people who cannot cope with it. They condemn the modern meritocracy that they cannot keep up with and cannot deal with. They become "obstructers" and continually question whether things are really needed. Most of these people will find jobs within the economy that suit their capabilities. However, there will, unfortunately, be others who will no longer be able to cope with the world and with change. They will quite simply blame society or globalization for this. Are the growing problems with marginalized people, drug addicts or high suicide rates the price we pay for a rapidly changing economically successful society?

## 3.4   The Goal Is Flexibility

Every person's goal should be to remain flexible. We shouldn't consider innovations a burden but rather view them positively and accept them as things that improve our circumstances. The goal of every company, and indeed every country, should be to develop a culture that embraces and strives for change. In an ever-changing world, those who do not keep up will be left behind.

There is the danger that a well-established profitable company will rest on its laurels and fail to renew itself by investing in either its employees or in research and development. Perhaps the employees also resist change and the new mindset associated with it simply because they are doing well. However, the competition will continue to do research and make investments. Initially, their growing lead will be imperceptible and gradual; their products or services will become cheaper and better. Meanwhile the products of the stagnating company become obsolete and the company begins losing market share and sales. This applies to companies as well as to entire economies. Over time, revenues will no longer cover costs. When reserves have been depleted, there is a threat of company closure or economic collapse. This is when employees and trade unions call for job-saving measures—and federal aid. And it is true that the company will survive for the time being if such action is taken. However, it will be increasingly difficult to fund the investments necessary for improvement. Meanwhile the competition will continue to invest in itself and improve, increasing the gap between the two types of companies. Federal aid becomes disproportionate or ineffective. There are only two options left. One is that the state takes over the business, thereby wasting taxpayers' money on an unprofitable operation. In the process, it runs the risk of going bankrupt itself if it takes over too many such businesses, especially since the free economy is becoming increasingly more efficient in other regions. The other option is that the business could be fundamentally restructured, which is only possible through the implementation of painful measures. The lack of continuous renewal, as would have been done by a healthy, competitive business, must be offset in a single step.

Maintaining an existing company structure leads to disadvantages in competitiveness. It bears repeating that only those who continually renew and work on their products and services and continually monitor and streamline costs will remain competitive and maintain economic health. Only those who embrace innovation and create a culture where change is welcome will stay on top.

If jobs are lost as a result of restructuring, there will, of course, be an outcry from those affected. Although this is understandable, such measures are, as a rule, economically necessary to ensure that the company survives. In an economy strengthened by continuous change, many new jobs are also created. However, this is reported much less dramatically in the media.

## 3.5  Impact on Entire Regions

Competition stimulates the economy in other ways. Companies in the same field of operation doing business in the same location can compete in such a way that they become industry leaders. Consider, for example, the former automobile industry in Detroit (USA), the chemical industry in Basel (Switzerland), Southern Germany's car industry featuring three global brands, both large banks in Switzerland, and many others. The oft-raised demand that such companies should join forces on the world market in order to avoid unnecessary competition with each other stems from a desire for convenience. Its proponents fail to recognize that the driving force behind the success of companies would be eliminated if this were done. Trends toward such convenience have often been followed by decline.

This is similar to the phenomenon seen in cartels, which also create a comfortable buffer, tempting them to neglect the constant striving for improvement and innovation. If a cartel fails, the companies affected are no longer competitive. They must either carry out improvements in a single step or undergo painful restructuring. When cartels fail, there are always winners and losers. The winners are those who are flexible, create better products and services, and enter new markets. In short, they take advantage of the opportunity. The losers are those who continue to sit back, complain that they can no longer exist, and then ask for federal aid. Antitrust laws have been tightened in many regions ensuring that lively competition is maintained.

# Chapter 4
# The Market, Market Failures, and Market Interventions

## 4.1 Competition as a Battle

Humans want to discover and dominate. Competition and innovation have always been the driving forces behind development. However, competition should not go so far as to lead to the destruction of mankind, whose preservation, obviously, is essential. In the days when individual tribes or clans fought, killed, or conquered each other, mankind was not endangered. Nor was its survival threatened when nations went to war. This changed with the introduction of nuclear weapons. We must hope that for the sake of our self-preservation, conflicts can be settled in a manner which does not compromise our survival[1] or destroy the foundations of life on this planet. Because humans are the only living creatures who can destroy themselves, it would, of course, be better if military conflicts could be avoided entirely. When going to war, we must be conscious of this.

Mankind must find a way to limit its urge to fight and engage in conflict to methods which are tolerable for everyone. This requires the rule of law as well as international norms, which are respected and can be enforced.

One aspect of conflict is competition. Economic warfare has replaced traditional warfare and satisfies the human need to fight and conquer. Considering the brutality of modern weapons, it is vital that mankind's propensity to fight and conquer be limited to economic conflict. Liberalism and international laws make this possible.

The readiness to fight when in competition stands in direct contrast to the human tendency towards lethargy or comfort. These characteristics contradict each other and are in constant conflict. Sometimes the desire to compete or fight prevails; sometimes the desire for comfort does.

---

[1]When a clan that is currently in power perceives its downfall to be inevitable, there is the danger that out of malice it will drag others down with it to destroy them i.e. accepting or even striving for the downfall of mankind. For example, if the regime in North Korea were on the brink of collapse, it might well use the atomic bomb, causing the destruction of all mankind.

© The Author(s) 2020
M. Meyer, *Liberal Democracy*, SpringerBriefs in Political Science,
https://doi.org/10.1007/978-3-030-47408-9_4

## 4.2   Optimizing Supply to Meet Demand

Every consumer has a purchasing power corresponding to his or her income. If consumers can use their funds freely, they buy what they consider to be the best; they receive the most for their money. Producers or suppliers, on the other hand, want to meet existing demands. If they are also free when designing their products and services, they will best be able to meet the demand. Theoretically an absolutely free market leads to the optimization of supply and demand and consequently to the greatest possible prosperity for society.

However, the market is in a state of flux. Products and service are continually being improved. Production, work, and leadership methods in companies also change, which in turn leads to an improvement or an optimization of the range of goods and services on supply. And finally, consumer needs change and with them the demand for products and services. Therefore, the optimal relationship between supply and demand is not a static parameter. Rather it is in a constant state of flux and must continually be adjusted. Products and services come, are improved, replaced by other products, or are pushed out of the market. Demand changes according to customer needs, their purchasing power, or simply according to trends.

The market steers not only supply and demand but also resources. Wherever products are successfully manufactured, the investment in labor and capital pay off. It is here that investors can allocate additional funds and employers can pay good salaries. The region can flourish. On the other hand, companies that fail to modernize run the risk of being overtaken by the competition causing a downward trend, which soon leads to an economic crisis.

## 4.3   Objective Market Failure

There is no such thing as an absolutely free market. The optimal business relationship between supplier and consumer is influenced by market interventions that are justified by *market failures*. We differentiate between objective market failure and subjective market failure. Objective market failure occurs when, for technical reasons, the market mechanisms do not allow the most favorable business climate. Subjective market failure, on the other hand, occurs when market mechanisms lead to a result that we do not want for political reasons because it doesn't meet our expectations of what we feel is "fair" or "right".

*Objective* market failure was at the root of the 2008 financial market crisis. The market mechanism in the capital and money markets was no longer leading to optimal results. The state intervened with guarantees, with aid to banks and with measures taken by the central bank. Market distortions are also caused by customs duties, difficult access to the labor market, quotas, or subsidies i.e. when the producer of a product or service benefits from government services and no longer has to bear the cost of producing alone. This includes basic research done by universities, if this research not only serves the general public but individual businesses as well. Other points included in this category involve environmental restoration by the state if it involves correcting damage done during the production of a product. If the cost of restoration is not borne by the producer in keeping with a "polluter-pays" principle or corrected by banning environmentally hazardous substances, then the market will be distorted. Failing to do so yields profits that are not based on performance but on a supported market.

The state should intervene in the case of such market failures. These interventions are justified if they result in a better allocation of costs and lead to market restoration. Examples of such interventions include the Cartel Act, which largely prevents price agreements as well as legal guarantee regulations, regulations on product information, or general business conditions that diffuse asymmetrical information availability, which can lead to market distortions when one market participant knows more than the others.

However, interventions always impede absolute free trade, even in the case of objective market failure. The consumer pays for this through higher prices. Both their purchasing power and their prosperity decreases. If, due to market regulations (for example, those for environmental protection), the most suitable producer no longer manufactures products in the cheapest region, competitiveness suffers which, in turn, reduces the purchasing power of the consumer.

## 4.4 Subjective Market Corrections

There are diverse *subjective* reasons for implementing the many price-increasing measures that affect the cheapest products. Often the results of the free market are deemed unfair and not politically acceptable. Such market interventions are based on a consideration of interests. The overarching interest in a functioning free market and the resulting maximum possible prosperity is weighed against the specific interest that serves as the basis for the market intervention.

Numerous interests justify such market interventions. We know that the free market leads to injustices that must be remedied. For this reason, the imposition of actions within the *social sector* to protect the welfare of the poor, the weak, and minorities is justified.

Other market interventions are implemented because people prefer convenience, reject efforts to change, and look for opportunities to gain advantages outside of competition. They try to regulate the market for their own benefit. This type of market intervention is increasing dramatically. When they occur, *we must remain aware that every market intervention will lead to a decrease in prosperity that will have to be paid for by everyone.* Well-developed countries in particular tend to lean towards regulation during economic booms by carelessly weighting other values and restricting the freedom of trade and industry. They argue that things are going well and they can afford to do so. This has resulted in the creation of labor laws, tenancy rights, planning rights, building and industry norms, tariff regulations, laws governing shop opening times, and other such laws as well as agricultural regulations and much more. They all have the potential to raise prices.

There are organizations that wish to support the privileges of their members outside the realm of competition. In most cases, these organizations do not contribute to prosperity for everyone. On the contrary, they influence the distribution of funds outside of market mechanisms by giving their members more than they have earned. This is always to the detriment of others and ultimately to the detriment of the general level of prosperity. Trade unions in different European countries provide a striking example of this. With their shows of force (strikes, blocking traffic, etc.) they thwart all attempts to reduce the privileges of their members. However, if labor laws are too rigid, the economy becomes rigid as well and won't be able to adapt its structures to new market conditions. Departments which are no longer profitable cannot be closed due to laws protecting workers from dismissal and new, future-oriented activities will not be sufficiently fostered out of fear of being trapped in this new structure later. The prosperity of the entire country suffers—and ultimately the prosperity of unionized workers as well.

Eastern Europe during the communist era provides another noteworthy example. The planned economy, combined with the privileges granted to bureaucrats, led to a rigid societal system that could not be restructured. The economy stayed around the same level that prevailed after World War II. Differences between East and West became increasingly larger until the system collapsed. Now, with tremendous effort these countries are making up for lost opportunities.

There are also organizations that defend the privileges of their members at the expense of the economy as a whole. Lawmakers have recognized cartels as being an obstacle to competition and have limited them in the interest of the national economy. Other interest groups such as industry and professional associations or labor unions are tolerated. These organizations seek to gain advantages for their members outside of the competitive arena by influencing political institutions.

Finally, various European countries support maintaining structures in individual sectors (for example, agriculture). The following is true of all organizations that wish to maintain the status quo: the more a country is affected by organizations intent on preserving a given structure, the less a country is able to adapt existing structures to new conditions and the more likely the country will fall behind in its ability to stay competitive. In older, more stable economies, there is a danger of developing an increasing number of such organizations and an increasing number of rules and regulations, thereby losing the initial dynamic which led to success. Countries which have enjoyed long-term stable conditions are particularly at risk of losing their powers of renewal.

It bears repeating: any type of market intervention leads to a higher level of prices (initially unnoticeable). *The sum of market interventions is reflected in the general level of prices and determines the standard of living in an economy.* The opportunity provided by change is limited by the degree of regulation within a society. Whether or not an economy can maintain or even increase its powers of renewal and its prosperity can be seen in the density of its rules and regulations. The more highly regulated a region is, the more prices will rise and the further the level of prosperity will fall.

Government is repeatedly tempted to intervene in order to preserve structures. The results are always the same: Protection leads to a short-term reprieve, which allows those affected to relax. Meanwhile the difference to unprotected competing companies in other countries or in other regions continues to grow. The burden on the government will become too expensive and the protective measures removed. The affected industry has to try to make up for missed opportunity and may even go under. Catching up will require a great deal of effort and there will be casualties.

## 4.5 Outdated Value Systems

There are dreamers who hold on to previous value systems although they have not stood the test of time and have long since become obsolete. Religious value systems are outdated even if the clergy in most religions continue to defend their authority. Some leftists still dream of socialism; their ideas appear periodically on the political surface when they speak of "overcoming capitalism". They cite injustices in their argumentation and demand equality without realizing the inequality socialism has created all over the world. Often these politicians are driven by envy or they are pursuing their own political careers. Yet the centralized socialist state has long since been replaced by a free market system.

200 years ago, the German philosopher Hegel,[2] in his description of dialectics, noted how value systems develop. A political thesis is juxtaposed with an antithesis. From this, a synthesis emerges as a compromise. This, in turn, becomes a thesis as soon as it is juxtaposed with an antithesis creating a new synthesis and so on. The development of value systems proceeds in steps moving forward; never backwards. Similarly, evolution leads to new mutations, which as a rule are better suited to life than previous ones. Evolution never returns to previous forms.

So, when searching for the way into the future and for the value system of that future, we have to start with the present system and check which antithesis is emerging. Will the information age or data age follow the free market system? Or will it be the age of robots and artificial intelligence? And what is the synthesis of these?

Do we want to *return to socialism*? The word "return" already suggests that it would be a step backwards. Socialism has failed too often. Failed economic systems all over the world (e.g. the Soviet Union, Venezuela, Cuba, the German Democratic Republic) testify to this. There is not one single example of a socialist system that was successful and led to more equity. Of course, it is within the rights of every individual and it is a consequence of the freedom of opinion that every person be

---

[2]Georg Wilhelm Friedrich Hegel (1770–1831).

allowed to hold onto old systems. However, the intellectual left's infatuation with yesterday's failed value systems does nothing to advance humanity.

Competition has always spurred us on to greater performance. Why then does socialism still enjoy a certain amount of popularity—especially among young intellectuals? Often these people have come to a theoretical conclusion (i.e. intellectual): they emotionally associate profit maximization with the oppression of the weak, whereas in their eyes socialism emphasizes social issues and justice. They therefore reason that socialism is better. They are not willing or are not mature enough to examine the evidence neutrally. Instead, they highlight facts that support their point of view but ignore or even suppress evidence that proves the opposite. Meanwhile, they continue to benefit from the prosperity that the free market economy brought them. In other words, their behavior contradicts their beliefs.

Our perceptions are rarely based on rational evidence. They are influenced by our human network—by the value system of the people around us. Individuals tend to conform to the value system of the group to which they belong and adopt its preferences. This is true for everything from the type of music preferred by social cliques in schools to the type of clothing or food that expresses social identity, to the anti-vaccination stance, which is often religiously influenced, and on up to socialism. Surprisingly, these value systems are sometimes used to justify and support social injustices. However, they do not promote truth.

The truth about a market economy can only be established if we analyze the system without pre-conceived values or prejudices, thereby understanding it and its advantages and disadvantages without being influenced by the environment and the value system we live in.

The free market economy has brought us a degree of wealth never before seen in history. Europeans have already developed this system further. Enormous redistribution mechanisms mean that hardly anyone has to make an effort to live in dignity. The original form of capitalism has become a social market economy. The welfare state seems to have found broad recognition in all European countries. Its existence no longer relies on a political party—the social democrats. Rather it is supported by all parties and a broad section of the population. In this regard, there are no longer left-wing or right-wing parties. Instead, political debates revolve around the degree of government involvement. Should there be "more government or less government"? No other form of government has brought society a higher level of satisfaction than the welfare state. This is one of the reasons that social democratic parties are shrinking—their goals have been realized and the political party is no longer needed. However, satisfaction also brings lethargy. Therefore, we have to continue working on the concept of the free market economy—even if it means tedious discussions with leftist intellectuals.

## 4.6  Globalization

The liberal value system combined with the market economy requires an international network—i.e. globalization. It enlarges the market area, promotes competition, and helps consumers purchase better products at lower prices. In turn, it also gives innovative market players greater opportunities improving everyone's level of prosperity. International competition—globalization—helps all participating regions. Prosperity increases internationally.

One aspect of globalization is not given enough emphasis: when nations compete with each other economically and win or lose with different products and services, they are engaged in an economic conflict, which largely replaces military conflict, making war less likely. Global economic conflict is replacing warlike conflict and is preventing war among economically progressive nations. Countries that are doing well do not wage war. They stand to lose too much and risk putting their national prosperity in danger. However, this requires that autocrats do not try to change the rules of the game or try to provoke foreign policy tensions for their own national political reasons. This is also why democracies are necessary for peace in prosperity.

## 4.7  Losers as Prey for Autocrats

Globalization also has its losers. In most cases, more successful companies will replace those that have lagged behind. Prosperity is maintained or even increased. However, social safety nets are needed wherever people are negatively affected by change, so that they can receive the necessary help to be reintegrated into the labor market. Most European countries do a great deal in this respect.

For lack of alternatives, those who lose at globalization or in our meritocracy fall back into old value systems—such as nationalism or into structures based in religion. They long for an autocratic system because they believe they will be more comfortably protected. People in less well-educated regions or in regions with high levels of unemployment tend to vote for nationalism and it is the more regressive religious societies which turn to fundamentalist beliefs. For centuries, nationalists and members of fundamentalist religions have not tolerated those who deviate from their beliefs and have fought those who do not belong to their community of values. They do not accept those who think differently and protect their own ideologies with violence or even war. Because they cannot keep up technologically, they are among the losers. They fight all those they consider to be on the other side with the simple, brutal methods of terrorism. They face a highly technological world with not only drones and electronic warfare, but also the temptations of freedom. They cannot win the conflict in the long run. A solution to this asymmetrical struggle has yet to be found. It most likely lies in better education in these regions.

Totalitarian countries such as Russia, Turkey, or Saudi Arabia encourage people to return to the previous value systems of autocratic governments or religions. These governments falsely represent themselves as democracies albeit oftentimes with manipulated elections. Such countries support political parties or movements in countries that are losing at globalization and which favor autocratic systems. Russia's use of manipulative political propaganda in the West or Saudi Arabia's and Turkey's support of local mosques is an example of such efforts. Claims by Vladimir Putin or leaders in China that suggest that liberalism is obsolete because it is losing to their system are also part of this manipulation. This assertion is not intended to strengthen their own people, but their own positions as autocrats. Such claims are absurd and are refuted by statistics. Economically, Russia lags far behind the West, and China will never completely catch up with—much less surpass— democracies. Doing so requires freedom. The assertion is even more absurd because the course of history never reverses. We have had more than enough autocratic countries since the Middle Ages. The trend is toward freedom and democracy.

# Chapter 5
# All People Are Winners

## 5.1 Prosperity Is Increasing Worldwide

Liberalism has brought people freedoms and levels of prosperity that have never before existed. This is true both for rich Western and Asian countries and countries that were previously poor. It is a long-term positive development that has always had to deal with setbacks.

Up until the eighteenth century, most people in Europe lived in severe poverty. They had no running water, no sewage systems, no medical care and hardly enough to eat. Many died of starvation, disease, or epidemics. Only the very rich—the aristocrats—did reasonably well. At that time, people in Europe lived no differently than people in the poorest countries in the world do today.

But it's not only the people living in developed first-world countries who are enjoying a level of prosperity never before experienced by mankind. The standard of living has risen everywhere else as well. Only in a few of the poorest countries are there people still dying of starvation and according to the UN Agenda 2030 from 2015,[1] extreme poverty should be eradicated within a few years. This forecast states that 380 million Africans will still be among the poorest, while elsewhere around 50 million people will continue to be affected by poverty. This is less than 6% of the world's population. Asians in particular will be able to escape poverty, while in Central Africa (and, depending on armed conflicts, in Middle Eastern countries) the number of people living in extreme poverty will increase. In these regions there are far too many refugees who are fleeing wars, economic crises, policy failures and—by extension—poverty and hunger.

---

[1]Resolution of the UN General Assembly adopted on 25 September 2015 Nr. 70/1. "Transforming our world: The Agenda 2030 for sustainable development". https://www.un.org/Depts/german/gv-70/band1/ar70001.pdf

In all other "poor" countries there is no longer any starvation.[2] In these countries, 60% of all girls attend school. 88% of the children have been vaccinated and 85% of the people have electricity. In general, it can be said that about 80–90% of the world's population can meet their basic needs. Therefore, real progress has been made all over the world.

## 5.2   Previously-Poor Regions Also Benefit

Time and again, it has been claimed that capitalism increases prosperity in developed countries while exploiting developing countries. However, as a quick look at the globe shows, developing countries that have a market economy combined with good governance (Chap. 11) stand a genuine chance of joining the ranks of the successful nations. Japan, Singapore, South Korea, and Taiwan have all achieved this within one or two generations. Many so-called emerging markets such as India and Brazil are well on their way to doing so. The same holds true for China if they change their systems and introduce good governance. Others believe they have been left behind. They speak of a first world elite who have mastered new technologies and are driving them forward, increasing the distance to those left behind and leaving them no opportunity to catch up. They fail to recognize the culpability of members of their own corrupt governments, who enrich themselves rather than invest in infrastructure and good governance.

Thousands of years ago, mankind began at the lowest level of prosperity. Gradually, the situation improved. However, even in the eighteenth century, many Europeans went to bed hungry and it took generations for prosperity to come. Poor countries are making progress more quickly today and it takes only a few generations to move from one level of prosperity to the next.

According to the IMF, the poorest countries have the highest rates of growth (2–6%—sometimes even higher). Wealthy countries are growing considerably more slowly (2–4%). Eventually, the poor countries will catch up. Provided they have developed a liberal democracy, income levels will equalize. What will happen then? People from previously poor countries are used to hard work and these countries will overtake the rich ones—until they have gotten used to prosperity (for example, Japan). Here too, development comes in waves. Many ambitious Europeans have already noticed that they have more opportunity in Asia than in Europe because growth rates are better. As a result, they are trying their luck there.

In addition:

- Average life expectancy is continuously increasing. In 1900, men born in Germany lived an average of 46.4 years and women 52.5 years. Today men are

---

[2]The figures in this chapter are based on the highly recommended book, *FACTFULNESS (Ten reasons we're wrong about the world and why things are better than you think)* by Hans Rosling.

expected to live 78.4 years and women 83.2 years. For most people on the planet, the average life expectancy has risen sharply.[3]

- When considered over the long-term, the difference between rich and poor is decreasing. In the past it was much more extreme. Until the eighteenth century, the rich had sovereignty over the poor rural population who were tied to the land and held as slaves. Since then, the difference between the two has continuously been reduced and statistics show that in most countries this continues to be the case.[4] Of course, there have also been setbacks, but the long-term development is clear and very positive.
- Crime, when considered from a long-term perspective, is decreasing.[5]
- War deaths are also declining, despite possible impressions to the contrary from the Middle East.
- Attitudes to war have changed considerably. In ancient Greece, death in battle was necessary to gain access to the afterlife. Napoleon was considered a hero, whereas Hitler was a criminal. During World War I, soldiers went enthusiastically to war, writing "On to Paris" on the railway wagons that carried them. They spoke of "Fields of Honor". Today if there is war, it is considered a crime.
- Epidemics are decreasing or they rarely occur anymore. In 1918, the Spanish Flu killed 2.7% of the world population. At the beginning of 2009, the Swine Flu lasted 2 weeks killing 31 people. Action taken thanks to global cooperation, modern medicine and technology will hopefully limit fatalities from the coronavirus.
- Since 1990, child mortality rates among children under the age of five have decreased by more than half, from 12.5 million children to 5.3 million in 2018. More than 80 countries, including many of the poorest, have been able to reduce child mortality rates by two thirds since 1990. (UNICEF Report, September 2019)

As Hans Rosling points out in his book, *FACTFULNESS*, many people do not see the progress that has been made. They lack a *fact-based* perspective. This could be because they are using outdated information; they are not familiar with the correct facts; or because they ignore facts that do not agree with their world view. Here is an

---

[3]Life expectancy has more than doubled since the 1870s. Here's a detailed link: https://de.statista.com/statistik/daten/studie/185394/umfrage/entwicklung-der-lebenserwartung-nach-geschlecht/.
During the Middle Ages, the average life expectancy for women was 25 years and for men 32 years. There is more information here: https://www.google.ch/search?q=Lebenserwartung+historisch&sa=X&ved=2ahUKEwjw946QrKHmAhVjwqYKHcnzAcoQ3rMBKAJ6BAgNEAk&biw=1745&bih=850

[4]Source: The statistics for "Standard of Living and Inequality of Income Distribution in Selected European Countries" from the Swiss Federal Office of Statistics, which refers to Eurostat—EU-SILC 2015 (Version from March 28, 2017), or the article from the Neu Zuericher Zeitung "Income Differences are Decreasing". (https://situation-bevoelkerung/soziale-situation-wohlbefinden-und-armut/ungleichheit-der-einkommensverteilung.html).

[5]Source: Swiss Police Crime Statistics https://www.bfs.admin.ch/bfs/de/home/aktuell/neue-veroeffentlichungen.assetdetail.7726202.html

example of outdated information from the late 1990s: In 1997, 42% of the world's population lived in extreme poverty. In 2019 only 9% did. In the last 20 years the number of people living in extreme poverty has decreased by half. Although the majority of people do not enjoy the same standard of living as the middle class in wealthy countries, they have enough to eat, their young girls can attend school, and their children receive basic medical care and are vaccinated. Step by step, conditions in the world are improving.

In summary, most people (80%) can now meet their basic needs. There are the very wealthy regions (Europe, North America, Japan, South Korea, Taiwan, Singapore); and there are extremely poor regions (about 9%) with unacceptable living conditions.[6]

Everything has improved!—What counts are the facts and not personal perception. Liberalism has increased prosperity almost everywhere in the world.

---

[6]The largest nutritional problem in the world today is not malnutrition but overnutrition, the urge to overeat by consuming fat and sugar resulting in obesity. We must teach children to avoid sweets and chips because there are too many of these and because of the enormous problem of food waste.

# Chapter 6
# Undesirable Developments and Possibilities for Improvement

## 6.1 Avoiding Undesirable Developments

Can we learn from history?

Evolutionary development does not stand still. It continues, albeit in very small steps, which often go unnoticed. Can we trace this development, identify it, and assign it a direction? Can we then project this trend into the future and hazard a forecast? Or was the past development random without any recognizable trend, making it impossible to make a prediction? We don't know.

However, what we can do is perceive how humans change outwardly. With every generation the average height has increased so that today, a young person cannot walk upright through the doorways of medieval castles. Although it has not been statistically proven, it also seems that the willingness to engage in physical altercations is decreasing. At any rate, long-term observation indicates that crime is on the decline.[1] Apparently, in the past, insults and other affronts were met with brutal beatings, whereas today compensation will most likely be sought. The brain mass of Neanderthals was roughly one-third of the brain mass of modern humans. Will the size of the brain continue to increase? Will humans evolve into even more intelligent beings? Will they become more altruistic and peaceful? Are we evolving in the desired direction?

The market economy, at any rate, has continued to evolve. In combination with basic rights and democracy it has led us to enormous freedom and prosperity. In accordance with Hegelian dialectics, one value system follows the next, with each system building on the existing one and continuing from there. Liberalism is evolving and improving.

But, of course, a liberal system also makes mistakes. It creates misguided incentives and inequalities, which must be addressed. I will discuss potential improvements in the next chapters.

---

[1]Please refer to Hans Rosling's statistics in Sect. and also the Swiss Police Crime Statistics.

© The Author(s) 2020
M. Meyer, *Liberal Democracy*, SpringerBriefs in Political Science,
https://doi.org/10.1007/978-3-030-47408-9_6

## 6.2   Erosion of the Middle Class

In some Western countries, middle class prosperity has decreased in recent years. This has affected Southern European countries (including France) and the USA. In Germany, the eastern part of the country has not yet reached the standard of the western part, which is causing dissatisfaction.

The purchasing power of the middle class is eroding because of the increased burdens being placed upon its members. They bear these by paying higher taxes. In the last 20 years many welfare states have doubled their expenditures. Policies have assigned more responsibilities to the state and these must be financed. This has led to an astonishing increase in tariffs and taxes, which have surpassed the "tithe" (usually 10%) that was paid to sovereigns in the Middle Ages. In some countries the level is already as high as 40% or even 50%.

Whenever the middle class has less and less, its loyalty to democracy and society decreases. A sense of community is lost and demands on the government increase. If these demands are not met, the tendency to fall for the promises made by autocrats or to try out other political systems or political parties increases. This can be seen in France where the *Gilets Jaunes* (Yellow Vests) are fighting against a decline in their standard of living. Or as seen in Italy (Spring/Summer 2019), when the Italian citizens no longer knew who they should vote for in order to stop a downward spiral. As a result, left-wing comedians formed a government with right-wing populists despite having very different views and no idea about economics. They both simply wanted power.

A free secular state thrives on conditions which it cannot guarantee.[2] It cannot use legal constraints and authoritarian dictates to prevent internal regulatory powers from moving in an anti-democratic direction without itself becoming an autocratic system. Admittedly, it is the task of a democracy to protect itself from such regulatory tendencies by enforcing its democratically adopted laws through the use of constitutional measures (courts, police). But what if the purpose of regulation is to limit the power of the rule of law and to undermine the separation of powers?

Because the middle class has such a strong majority, such situations endanger democracy. The middle class is democracy's most important supporting pillar; therefore, the strengthening of this class must be a political and moral goal.

The erosion of the middle class can be attributed to *misguided developments*. These include government that is far too expensive with an excessively high government ratio, as well as over-regulation with excessive bureaucracy and too much redistribution. As a result, infrastructure and schools are neglected. I will address these issues in the following chapters.

---

[2]Ernst-Wolfgang Böckenförde (1930–2019), Constitutional Court judge in Germany. This thought was first expressed in a speech in the summer of 1964.

## 6.3 Leaner Government

The *government ratio* expresses total government expenditures as a percentage of gross domestic product (GDP). It has risen continuously in all European countries. However, international comparisons are not relevant here because they are based on different statistics. What is more important is *the development over the years in individual countries*—the "track record". This development shows the level of deterioration compared to earlier conditions and the resulting pressure which is put on the level of prosperity. One aspect becomes quite clear: there are not fewer people working for government and there are not fewer people who are financially dependent on it than in earlier times. Rather, each year there are more people who depend on the government for their existence. The state is not spending less, it is increasingly spending more. This government growth is being driven by an entitlement mentality, which is frightening and does not bode well for the future.

Governments should use revenue primarily to develop infrastructure and to ensure the safety of its citizens. These are the foundation of prosperity. Today, some types of infrastructure are considered basic human rights. This includes a good school system available to everyone. It also includes well-developed transportation routes, electricity supply, the best communication systems possible, a safe water supply, refuse collection and much more. Only when all of these things work well and efficiently can the level of prosperity grow.

Shifts in the balance of power between social groups having different views about government are fatal—especially if there is an increase among groups which are anti-competitive. These shifts occur when too many people depend on a "strong state" to guarantee their existence. One such example can be found in Italy. If about 60% of the gross national product flows into the government budget and is then redistributed within the state, it becomes almost impossible to push through reforms. Any reforms would be at the expense of the beneficiaries, who are in the majority. On the other hand, the minorities who are responsible for value creation—those working in commerce, industry and small and medium-sized businesses are being exploited. For them, the state is an enemy to which they owe no allegiance. Another example is seen in France, where age-old structures allow little room for reform.

Not all government expenditure is used for the administration of the state or is relevant for value creation (expenditure for infrastructure, etc.). A large part is transfer payments, which redistribute revenues generated in various economic sectors and include subsidies, tax incentives, and aid to entire segments of the economy, all of which are included in government expenditure. It is precisely these that have risen disproportionately and contribute significantly to increases in the government ratio.

## 6.4   Deregulation

Economic success depends on the business *environment*. This could not be more different in each country. *Regulatory density* makes up a part of this environment. Whether entrepreneurs have to observe a number of laws or only a few for their types of activity, or whether they have to obtain several or only a few permits, or whether they have to pay high or low fees will have an impact on business. *Regulatory density* is decisive when it comes to success or failure. It can also be said that in the meantime there are now so many laws it is impossible to obey them all.

How can regulatory density be reduced? A catastrophe creates the opportunity to build something new on the ruins. This was true when the dinosaurs became extinct. Thanks to their disappearance, it became possible for mammals and ultimately humans to evolve. The ancient Greeks depicted this as the "phoenix rising from the ashes" and the concept is still true today. If a region is destroyed by war, there are no structures or laws left to impede the fast and uncomplicated construction and development of a new and oftentimes more successful society. After the Second World War, government structures in Germany were largely destroyed. A new beginning could be made without obstructive, pre-existing regulations—the result of which was the German economic miracle. Victorious England, on the other hand, fell from being a world power to a regional one after Churchill was ousted as prime minister and the labor government began its long reign. A frenzy of regulations stifled the economy. It was only when Margaret Thatcher began rigorous deregulation that this changed.

Do we need a new catastrophe? Previously, every generation had its own war, which left behind ruins on which it was possible to rebuild. Long periods of peace lead to such a dense concentration of rules and laws that citizens and companies drown in paragraphs and fees, causing them to lose initiative and, as a result, prosperity begins to erode.[3] Let's hope we can find a way out of this vicious regulatory cycle without a catastrophe. Politicians have long promised to fight over-regulation. However, their apparent inability and failure to do so is frightening. We do not need a war, but as a substitute, we do need peaceful periodic deregulation. Not only does material law play a role here but also procedural law. Procedural restrictions are constantly being put in place and an increasing number of economic activities are now subject to permits. Why is there no resistance to this? Have we already become too complacent? How about creating a committee to identify and eliminate all measures which inhibit economic growth?[4] What about a provision which requires that before a new law can come into force, the same number or even twice as many existing provisions be deleted at the same time (this could be based on the number of words or preferably based on the costs incurred). How about introducing a provision that says that a new permit regulation can only be implemented if a permit regulation is lifted in another area?

---

[3]cf. Mancur Olson, "The Rise and Decline of Nations", New Haven and London, 1982.

[4]President Reagan did exactly this in the USA.

## 6.5   Redistribution

The burden of redistribution, which for a lengthy period has not been just from wealthy to poor, is no longer being borne by the rich, but primarily by the middle class.

A liberal welfare state lives from extreme redistribution—for pensions and pension schemes, homes for the elderly, for health care costs and social services, for daycare, for the agricultural sector, the energy industry, for environmental protection and much more. The revenue comes primarily from middle-class taxes. Other tax sources (e.g. a wealth tax) would be far too low. In the process, the redistribution apparatus swallows up a part of the revenues so that only a reduced amount (between 50% and 80%) of the money goes to the designated area.

The *redistribution* system needs improvement because it leads to dissatisfaction on all sides. The intention to promote the well-being of all has been successful to that extent that even the poorest people in highly developed countries benefit from the system and can afford to spend money on non-essential items. In many European countries, economic development has remained positive and the income gap between the rich and the poor has continued to decrease. (cf. Sect. 6.2). However, in other countries (in Southern Europe including France, and the USA) the income gap has begun increasing again in recent years. This has been especially true in European countries which are centrally organized, and whose central government (bureaucracy) grew overwhelmingly, resulting in a greatly increased government ratio. After all, someone has to pay for centralized government with the redistributions it entails.

Redistribution is necessary to maintain social order. However, it is not efficient. Too much money "evaporates" and, if the cost of redistribution is too high, it creates a dichotomy between those fleeing it and those who become complacent because of it. Misuse increases. In addition, when there is a high level of redistribution, it is often inefficient and results in a loss of community spirit among the middle classes. Expectations on the government rise—expectations which can hardly be fulfilled. As a result, more taxes are needed so that more can be redistributed.

Redistribution, in turn, creates discord and it is not the final stage with regards to developing a fair system. The poor only benefit if something is taken away from the rich. They do not create their standard of living by virtue of their own work or their own ideas, but rather to the "detriment" of others. This cannot be satisfying for anyone. The rich are forced to give away their wealth, which they usually find annoying regardless of the social justification behind it. Their resentment leads to countermeasures which do not contribute to a peaceful society as, for example, when billions of dollars are contributed to election campaigns to support the economic system of the rich (e.g. USA). And finally, redistribution involves tremendous bureaucracy, which no one wants at all.

The goal must be a society in which everyone can earn their own wealth. Wage systems have to allow each citizen to live decently and save for his or her retirement, pay for health insurance, and so on without redistribution and bureaucracy. We certainly feel it is fair to reward performance. Those who work more or contribute more to society should also earn more. We reject those profiteers, who only take from society (and thereby from those who contribute more) and contribute hardly anything themselves. A system of redistribution also harbors the danger of political dissatisfaction and disputes. Some people do earn too much, and others who work and contribute to society earn too little. This must be corrected. But calls for hatred of the rich do not help. Taking away from successful people and giving it to profiteers is not a long-term solution. Often the cries for redistribution do not help the poor who work and fight to get ahead. Rather they help profiteers who propagate envy and hate.

We must therefore seek a system in which fair wages are inherent without the need for additional state intervention and redistribution. We must create an economic system that pays fair wages so that the gap between rich and poor appears to be equitable, with each achieving his or her own standard. Redistribution will then be limited only to those who cannot take care of themselves (sick, disabled, etc.). The rich will gladly contribute money for these people.

An economic system which, by its very nature, has led to fair pay for all exists to some extent in the Nordic countries and in Switzerland. In these countries, the middle class is content and the gap between rich and poor continues to decrease. The system is not perfect, however, and I would recommend that research progress be made in this area as our future depends on the further development of liberalism.

## 6.6    A Good School System for Everyone (Equal Opportunity)

Equal opportunity is not always a reality even in highly developed countries. In the USA, for example, the gap between the rich and the poor has recently increased and the American dream in which it is possible for a dishwasher to become a millionaire is becoming increasingly more difficult to achieve. The educational system is probably to blame. Good schools must be paid for privately, which significantly improves the chances of children with wealthy parents compared to those whose parents are poorer.

Only where the educational systems are equally accessible to all is there also equal opportunity for all. Therefore, schools and universities should not be financed by tuition fees but by the state or by private educational organizations.

## 6.7    Excesses in Liberalism

Excesses in liberalism also exist—in two respects:

Some individual top executives earn a salary that is far in excess of their performance level. This disrupts peace within a political system. In fact, it actually destroys it. It is especially alarming when people obtain a high-ranking position, stay there for a few years, and become so rich they can resign. This gives the impression that they are only interested in increasing their own wealth over the course of a few years rather than working towards the good of the company and its employees.[5] Included in the list of grossly overpaid people are top athletes, for example in football or soccer, tennis, etc. although, these salaries tend to be more widely accepted than those of managers.

Another excess can be seen in "company trading". Far too much money is "earned" in asset management, i.e. the buying and selling of large share packages or entire companies. Some of the richest people in the world today made their money as fund managers or in the building up and selling of companies. This includes young people who grow a startup company for a few years and then sell it for millions of dollars, as well as companies that do well during the startup phase and then are sold on the stock market sometimes for billions of dollars.

The liberal system needs correction in both these areas.

## 6.8 Income Distribution

Income inequality has been greatly reduced since the Middle Ages and in modern times the trend continues to be positive globally. According to the statistics used here,[6] the trend in Europe has remained stable over the past few years. However, there are some who are of the opinion that inequality is increasing again, especially in France, Italy and Spain as well as in the USA. This is an unfortunate development that must be corrected (see Sect. 6.5 above "Redistribution").

The cause of this new inequality is the erosion of the middle class; as a consequence, both extremes—rich and poor—are increasing. The middle class must be made stronger by reducing the amount of government and the government ratio, reducing deregulation, and redistribution, etc. If the middle class is relieved of these tremendous burdens, they will become stronger and income disparities will decrease.

---

[5]With demands for excessive compensation, the greed of some managers in larger companies betrays and endangers the ethics on which our prosperity is based. This leads to attempts at regulation, which, in my country, the people agreed to in a referendum. Such regulations have remained largely ineffective. Are they useful? It would be better if managers voluntarily adhered to the ethic of "performance with humility".

[6]Swiss Federal Office of Statistics: https://www.bfs.admin.ch/bfs/de/home/statistiken/wirtschaftliche-soziale-situation-bevoelkerung/soziale-situation-wohlbefinden-und-armut/ungleichheit-der-einkommensverteilung.html

Some economists[7] and even some international organizations such as the OECD call for just the opposite, specifically more government and higher taxes for redistribution. These opinions stem from an environment of excessive central government, which only knows of solutions provided by government intervention and which searches for new tax sources to fund them. They demand tax alignment, i.e. tax harmonization from more successful competing countries with leaner structures and lower taxes because tax competition impedes their high tax policies. They ignore the fact that these other countries are more successful in their fight against income inequality and that the middle class in these countries is more content.[8]

Efforts by the OECD to tax international companies where their turnover is generated has also led to an "upward" tax harmonization because it helps high tax countries—which have lost business due to this—to increase revenues. These funds are then no longer available in the country where the business is domiciled. This in turn causes these countries to raise their taxes. Taxes are increased all around and countries with lean tax policies are penalized.

At the very most, the OECD's call for tax harmonization would be appropriate if all countries pursued sensible policies concerning their national budgets and government ratios. Unfortunately, this is not the case. There are countries that have a disproportionately higher government ratio and excessive bureaucracy. Financing these governments via tax harmonization with leaner countries is not only wrong, it hinders those states with more inefficient bureaucracies from finally restructuring themselves.

Tax competition and the competition between various types of administrative systems in general (see Sect. 10.4) help to keep taxes low and force administrations to become and remain more efficient. To this end, the people or companies concerned must be given the opportunity to choose the best environment and the best system in light of the competition for themselves. This is also true for tax competition, where it is certainly appropriate to "vote with your feet".[9]

---

[7]Thomas Piketty in *Capital in the Twenty-First Century* identifies rising income disparities as a major problem. Naturally such a development must be corrected. But to correct it he only suggests new taxes, for example a rigorous wealth tax, an inheritance tax or a global wealth tax. He does not even consider other economic measures.

[8]Despite what advocates of tax harmonization claim, the success of countries that do not have high tax policies cannot be attributed to companies moving there. Instead, it is the consequence of greater opportunity for small and medium sized companies (more freedom for spending and activities). The Swiss electorate has rejected a popular initiative for a wealth tax at the federal level and several times in various cantons, with apparently good results.

[9]"To vote with your feet" does not refer to voting by ballet, but to choosing to leave an area with a political system you disagree with in favor of an environment with the best political system for you.

## 6.9 More Individual Responsibility

Today we enjoy the highest level of freedom and the highest level of prosperity ever experienced in history. These are unique achievements and they are based on economic liberalism in conjunction with civil liberties. Yet it is alarming to see how many people are no longer aware of the foundations of our prosperity. They continually whittle away at these foundations with new initiatives and by placing demands on the government and society—actions that could actually destroy these foundations. It is especially the numerous activists in various areas such as organic farming, animal rights, women's rights, environmental protection, etc. who seem to know very little about or are completely unaware of these foundations. Do they not know that *it is not always necessary to have new laws for everything*? Wouldn't organic farming or other environmental demands be just as efficiently supported if consumers *used their freedom* to buy only what they consider to be responsible? Each new regulation limits freedom. Each new regulation increases regulatory density and ultimately limits prosperity. Are additional regulations and new restrictions on freedom really worth it?

People who moralize claim morality for themselves. They claim to have the only morally impeccable reasons for doing what they do and they insinuate that the opposite is true of others. They know exactly what is good and what is evil, and they consider themselves to be the good guys. They want to use laws to enforce what is good—laws which must be obeyed by everyone—even the evil ones. But are they really the good guys? Doesn't morality impose one-sided standards, which vary from culture to culture and person to person. Is morality considered to be so absolute that it can be claimed by everyone as a higher truth?

# Chapter 7
# Behavior Towards Autocracies

## 7.1 A Missionary in Economics?

Not all regions in the world have reached the same level of development. The question therefore arises: how should a successful democracy deal with autocratic nations?

First of all, it should be noted that it is not for us to impose our system on other nations. Even though we know that freedom, liberalism and democracy are pre-requisites for success, it is not our place to go forth with missionary zeal encouraging other nations to adopt our systems. All are responsible for their own happiness—not just every person but every country. However, there are limits to acceptable auto-cratic behavior and when these are exceeded, intervention is necessary.

Wherever the *market economy* does not work, it is up to each country to decide whether or not to leave things as they are even if this means it must accept a lower level of prosperity. Often such countries claim that strong centralized leadership is needed in order to catch up. However, this demands that an autocrat be honest and work for the common good. Delegation of power requires trust. Trustworthy auto-crats are difficult to find. They generally put their own power in the forefront and do everything they can to maintain it. They do not work to advance their countries—only themselves.

## 7.2 The Hierarchical System

Hierarchical systems can be found everywhere in nature. In herds there is a dominant or lead animal, i.e. a head bull, a wolf as leader of the pack, or a monkey as leader of the troop. They are hierarchical creatures used to authority. Obviously, this structure prevailed throughout evolution by ensuring that survival within the herd is easier than if each individual animal only looks out for itself. Herds would probably fall

© The Author(s) 2020
M. Meyer, *Liberal Democracy*, SpringerBriefs in Political Science,
https://doi.org/10.1007/978-3-030-47408-9_7

apart and cease to exist without this dominant or lead animal. Additionally, hierarchical systems satisfy the fight and dominate instinct, because the herd leadership position must be won, at times through very aggressive fights. In his best-selling book, *The Selfish Gene*,[1] Richard Dawkins, as the title suggests, describes genes as selfish and points out that this has been so since the beginning of evolution. Genes are selfish and they can exhibit this selfishness without evidencing any type of intelligence.

Humans, on the cutting edge of evolution, are also hierarchical and have taken on hierarchical leadership structures. Even groups of young people have leaders. Therefore, when autocrats claim that goals can be more efficiently reached through centralized leadership, it sounds credible.

Hierarchies appear in all parts of society. Football teams need a captain in order to win; armies need hierarchical structures in order to function well; even companies operating in the market economies of developed countries need strong central leadership as well as democratic leadership aspects to be successful. Therefore, it could be claimed that countries also need autocratic leadership in order to be successful.

Humans have always lived in hierarchical structures with emperors, kings, or dictators at the top. It doesn't matter how the leader came to power, whether through birth (inherited) or through a power struggle. It only matters that they are recognized as a leader within the value system of those being ruled. Obviously, this type of organizational structure is in our genetic makeup.

It is only within the last few centuries that hierarchical orders have come into question, particularly in Europe. Human rights demanded that everyone be treated equally; in other words, no one was superior to another person. For everyone living together to feel at ease, the rules require that everyone has a say. It is only when a group attempts to successfully achieve something together that a leader and—by extension—a hierarchy become necessary. And even in this case, there is a growing trend toward an egalitarian system. Bosses are no longer "always right". They must listen to the opinions of their subordinates or experts, weigh these and then make their decisions. Companies at either extreme—those run strictly democratically and those run as centralist authoritarian enterprises—cannot be successful. A combination of both is needed and the combination will depend on the needs and education of those concerned.

Questions then arise: is evolution continuing and are the people in democratic regions experiencing a period of growth? Did these people experience an evolutionary surge which has made them more altruistic and led them away from hierarchical orders?

At any rate one thing is clear: regions with democracies and human rights have more success economically than societies led by autocrats. And they are further along in their development. Wherever people accept an authoritarian regime (a king, a dictator) as a matter of course, the free market economy suffers. Such regions lag

---

[1]Richard Dawkins, *The Selfish Gene*, Oxford University Press, ISBN: 9780198788607.

behind in development when compared to constitutional democracies. This can be seen in Asia where democratic countries (Japan, Singapore, South Korea, Taiwan) are more successful in per capita income than China. The trend everywhere is from prosperity to well-being (see Sect. 2.4).

## 7.3  Limits for Autocrats

Autocracies always lag behind. But that is not a reason to intervene. Each country must decide for itself whether it is doing well under an autocratic ruler or if that ruler should be ousted. However, there are situations that justify intervention: for example, when such a leader is under pressure and begins to stage situations that they believe will unite the people in their favor, allowing them to stay on top.

If an autocratic ruler seeks foreign policy confrontations or even starts a war, democracies must respond harshly. They haven't interfered in the autocratic system in the past but may now demand that the autocracy refrain from interfering in other countries. This requires that highly developed countries *maintain their military power*. It also requires that they not waste time by continually insisting that "we have to talk". And it requires boundaries, which when compromised, are defended without compromise.

When theocracies wage war abroad, it is difficult to respond to their actions. When autocracies wage a propaganda war abroad in order to influence elections and destabilize the population there, and when they do not flinch at using their secret service agents to poison their opponents (Russia in England, North Korea in Malaysia, Saudi Arabia in Turkey), or to murder (Germany), they must be censured. Finally, when autocrats occupy foreign territory (Russia in Crimea, China in the South China Sea, Turkey in the Mediterranean), they must be confronted. It is regrettable and almost irresponsible that as an aftereffect of World War II, Europeans are no longer willing to use their authority to oppose such offenders and prefer to simply "talk". Rather than create an organization that can respond to attacks led by autocrats, they leave all decisive responses to the Americans. Demanding reciprocity with regards to religious tolerance (churches in Saudi Arabia) or with regards to economic freedom, freedom to own property, copyright, etc. is one of the obvious rules of engagement.

A distinction must be made when autocrats disregard *basic rights*. If it is a matter of basic rights not being allowed within the system (freedom of trade, the right to own property), it is difficult to intervene, and it would be difficult to justify. These countries must decide for themselves what is important for them. However, we can assume that young people all over the world are attracted to and inspired by the freedoms and rights experienced in democratic countries and will be motivated to demand the same system in their own countries.

If, however, individual rights are being violated, and this violation is punishable by law (injury to life and limb), then our conscience demands that we intervene. For instance, accusations of torture must be investigated, whether they are accusations in

Turkey or Iran, prison camps in Russia, or "re-education" camps in China. In particular, we cannot ignore reports of concentration camps in the Chinese province of Xinjiang, where apparently over one million prisoners of different faiths are being held.

The International Criminal Court plays an important role in this respect.

Barriers to intervention are much lower in countries that are close to us because we share similar values (often belonging to organizations such as NATO or the European Union). In this regard, human rights as well as conditions for "good governance" (separation of powers, no corruption, see Chap. 12) must be maintained without compromise. Here again, it is important not only that we talk about these principles; they must also be enforced. It is a shame that continental European countries tend to "talk" more in this respect. The English, with their uncompromising approach, would be important for Europe. For example, they investigated a poisoning in Britain by the Russian Secret Service and published the results of their investigation without any consideration of the Russian government.

# Chapter 8
# Xenophobia

## 8.1 There Has Always Been Migration

The first humans were hunters and gatherers who did not settle in one place. Can we conclude, accordingly, that migration is in our blood, that we always move on when a place has nothing left to offer? It was only later in history that developments such as agriculture would force humans to settle down so that they could harvest what had they had sown. The increase in population also led people to settle in villages and towns. As clans began to form tribes, relocation became more difficult. However, mass migrations during the first centuries demonstrate that entire populations continued to move. While these early migrations probably frightened the people who had already settled in an area, it would also have forced them out of their lethargy, quite likely leading to renewed momentum in the region.

Today there are also regions that are not used to dealing with immigrants. The locals fear a dilution of their own culture or they no longer feel safe and dare not go out at night; or they claim that they themselves are not well enough off to cope with immigration.

One problem with immigration is the value system immigrants bring with them. If too many of these values diverge from those of the host country (no sense of community, clan orientation, etc.), it can lead to a sense of alienation in the local population; this is especially true if immigrants are left among themselves to form "ethnic enclaves" such as Chinatowns, Turkish districts, etc. Immigrants have to be integrated, taught the local language, and included in work processes with the established residents. The second generation at the very latest should, through their attendance in local schools, be indistinguishable from the native population. Urban planning also has a role to play in laying the foundations for achieving this integration.

Immigration in social welfare systems endangers social stability and encourages populists to fight against it. However, the amount of money involved is not significant because the majority of young immigrants work hard and pay much more into

© The Author(s) 2020
M. Meyer, *Liberal Democracy*, SpringerBriefs in Political Science,
https://doi.org/10.1007/978-3-030-47408-9_8

the welfare system than less honest individuals, who only take from it. Misuse of welfare by immigrants can be countered with the same instruments used to combat abuse by local citizens.

## 8.2   The Positive Outweighs the Negative

Immigration not only helps refugees secure a better life, it also promotes innovation and flexibility in the region concerned. Immigrants tend to have more entrepreneurial spirit than the compatriots they left behind. But you would not necessarily know this when you see these poor people as they are fleeing their native lands. People often only realize it after immigrants have been integrated and taught the new culture. And this often can be clearly seen in the second generation.

As a Swiss, I don't want to emphasize our own expertise and have therefore chosen to say little about the successes and failures of my country in this book. However, when it comes to problems concerning immigration, I will make an exception. Switzerland has a great many foreigners living within its borders, and this has been the case for hundreds of years. On average, about 25% of the people living within Switzerland are foreigners. Larger cities like Zurich have a foreign population of over 25% and Geneva holds the record with a foreign population of over 33%.[1] This is higher than in most other European countries. Every year, many of these people are naturalized. However, with the annual arrival of new refugees, the number of foreigners continues to increase slightly each year. In the seventeenth century a wave of Huguenots came to Switzerland. They were French protestants who fled to Calvin in Geneva after a massacre in their home country. They later moved on to protestant cantons in Switzerland. At that time, there were no borders and no passports. Suddenly one-third of the Swiss population was made up of Huguenots. Like most immigrants, they sought peace and work. And the majority were hard-working people that were a great asset to the country. By the end of the nineteenth century, Italians had integrated en masse (the first Gotthard tunnel was largely built by Italians). They were later joined by Spaniards, Portuguese, immigrants from former Yugoslavia, northern Africa, Turkey, and Iran. Today in our trams and busses, we hear a colorful mixture of languages. Everyone, especially the Swiss, has grown accustomed to this.

Immigrants in Switzerland are integrated into our labor market; they have to learn at least one of our four national languages and their children attend school here. Most immigrants are eager to work and want to earn their own livings. Today, Italian-speaking immigrants are members of cantonal and national councils and "Italianità"

---

[1]Breakdown of the permanent resident population of Switzerland by Canton as of December 31, 2018 Office of Statistics: Switzerland 6,396,252 (74.857%); Foreigners 2,148,275 (25.142%). Geneva: Swiss 1,099,297 (66.925%), Foreigners 543,283 (33.075%); Zurich: Swiss 1,112,574 (73.149%), Foreigners 408,394 (26.850%).

has become a trend. Even immigrants from sub-Saharan Africa have become mayors of cities, and in an alpine city in Canton Vaud, a foreigner was elected president of the naturalization commission.[2] Some municipalities give foreigners voting rights at the local level based on the principle of "whoever pays taxes should have a say and bear responsibility". In this respect, the French-speaking part of Switzerland is leading the way. Zurich is also discussing extending voting rights at the local level to foreigners who have lived in Switzerland for more than 5 years. They argue that it is not acceptable to exclude 25% of the tax paying public from this responsibility. The CEO of one of the largest chemical companies in Basel is an Indian-American and until February 2020 the CEO of the second largest international bank in Switzerland (Crédit Suisse) was from sub-Saharan Africa. One thing that was always important was that Swiss identity not get lost. In fact, quite the opposite happened. Often immigrants appreciate and defend local customs much more than their local counterparts. Most of them have become good Swiss and have learnt to accept and appreciate the advantages of the country.

Switzerland has benefited greatly from immigrants. They have brought new ideas and helped increase the level of prosperity enormously.

## 8.3   Immigration Limits

Swiss people have expressed their views on immigration in several referenda. They have never banned it, but have restricted immigration to a very high level and have, in particular, ensured that the potential for integration is not jeopardized by the sheer number of immigrants coming into the country. After all, immigration is not a human right.

*Immigration must be objectively limited by a country's ability to integrate these new people.*

If foreigners can no longer be integrated, then immigration must be limited accordingly. Freedom of movement is indeed something that countries should strive for. However, it only works if the economic standards within the free movement zone are equal (as for example, in the USA). In this case, freedom of movement is only a question of who prefers to live where. If, however, the standard of living varies greatly, then regions with higher wages and salaries will be overrun. The EU experienced this with immigrants from Eastern European EU countries. Why should we prevent the influx of such immigrants and yet still emphasize freedom of movement as the cornerstone of the EU? Are we applying two different standards for the same problem?[3] If the EU had better understood the problem of

---

[2]The Commission makes recommendations at the municipal level concerning naturalization. Here the municipality has authorized the election of foreigners to its committees.

[3]Qualified immigrants weaken their country of origin (Brain Drain). For example, in countries such as Croatia, there are hardly any good craftsmen left.

immigration—especially from its own eastern countries—and had dealt with the issue earlier, it might have been able to defuse its subsequent problems with refugees as well. Perhaps the Brexit vote would have come out differently, especially as freedom of movement within the EU was a key issue (Brexit supporters argued that it had resulted in too many Polish immigrants in central England).

## 8.4   Politics with Immigration

Immigrants often arrive with new ideas; they are willing to work and want to build up a livelihood. Rarely are they motivated simply by profit. When they have learned the language and been integrated into the working world, the country benefits from them, at the latest with a second generation that has adapted completely to the new country.

Practicing politics at the expense of vulnerable foreigners—especially refugees who have often experienced terrible things—is dubious. It is easy for politicians to score points with xenophobia. Such politicians try to increase their influence by taking up this issue and providing simple solutions ("We don't want a flood of immigrants"). They are elected even though they do not have any qualifications other than their opposition to immigration. More specifically, most of them lack the requisite economic or business knowledge to lead their country toward economic growth. They then blame their lack of economic success on foreigners, using immigration to hide the fact that they are not really concerned about the good of the country, but only about their own political power.

Such politicians would do better to strengthen their countries' economic power. However, they usually lack the necessary skill to do this and use other issues to distract voters. Immigration is especially suited for this.

# Chapter 9
# Education and Culture Made the Difference

## 9.1 Education Shapes the Individual

For centuries, the Roman Empire extended to all areas around the Mediterranean (northern Africa, Arabia, Mesopotamia, Turkey, most of Europe and up to the middle of England). The people in this huge empire and most probably in the neighboring regions intermarried. For example, the legions stationed in one region had to come from a different part of the empire. As a result, the gene pool of all these people in the territory of the former Roman Empire will be similar (today this territory includes countries in and around Europe). From a statistical point of view every newborn has about the same genetic starting point and the distribution of intellectually, technically or manually skilled people is similar.

However, after birth, people develop differently. In particular, the brain develops according to how it is used. The parts of the brain which are used more often develop at a higher rate and become more agile than those areas that are rarely used. We also know that well into old age, new brain cells develop to strengthen areas of the brain that are heavily used. Should a part of the brain cease to function because of an accident, another part of the brain may take over its role. In doing so, it can grow, and new brain cells are created to fulfill this function. The brain of a person who has been taught and educated from the very beginning has trained the capacity to absorb knowledge. The brain of a person who has had to deal with violence from an early age can deal with it better. Education is important. If a person's brain has been exposed to education, it values its importance and is motivated to learn. Such people are more likely to take an interest in their own education and be committed to supporting education in their country as well.[1]

---

[1]Environment forms a person. If, for example, a person has been involved in intelligence work for a long time (Putin) their strengths will lie in this area and less so in conflict resolution without the use of intrigue. Knowledge about a person's early environment can also be used to assess a person.

© The Author(s) 2020
M. Meyer, *Liberal Democracy*, SpringerBriefs in Political Science,
https://doi.org/10.1007/978-3-030-47408-9_9

Education is provided in the form of schooling and is also embedded in the family and culture. Culture is a value system that defines opinions and rules of behavior that can accelerate, delay or even prevent development. Culture forms human beings.

## 9.2   Education as a Prerequisite for Prosperity

*Education is one of the most important prerequisites for prosperity and peace.* Only the best schools and educational systems in the world will lead to the highest possible standard of living. If education is neglected, a downward trend will begin.

Inertia in education—perhaps as a result of prosperity—is catastrophic.

Education and culture are also important in developing countries in order to ensure a successful path to prosperity. There are studies[2] that view culture in terms of values and norms of behavior and see it to be the deciding factor between successful nations and those that are not successful. Educated citizens are the foundation for prosperity because they question culture and do not see it as a God-given system of thought and behavior. In particular, culture should encourage entrepreneurship. If entrepreneurship is suppressed, prosperity is not possible. Ultimately, what is important is the spirit of innovation as well as work, thriftiness, honesty, patience and persistence—in other words, Calvinist ethics as we know them in Central and Northern Europe.

## 9.3   Regulatory Hurdles

As the average intelligence of all humans is the same at birth, difference in economic development cannot be attributed to genetic make-up (I am avoiding the word "race"). This difference is dependent on other factors such as education, culture, and infrastructure as well as all the other *basic conditions* offered by the government to those who aspire to develop themselves. Economic development depends on whether or not it takes only a few days, several weeks, or even several months to found a new company. It depends on whether entrepreneurs will encounter numerous regulatory obstacles or if they have to apply for numerous permits before they can finally start a business (for more on the effects of regulatory density on prosperity see Sect. 6.4).

---

[2]David Landes, *The Wealth and Poverty of Nations*, published by Little, Brown & Company.

## 9.4   Foundation for Democracy

Education provides an essential foundation for democracy. It is only when people can deal with a high degree of information and can understand the relationships between issues that they will be able to assess whether their decision will have a positive or negative effect on the future. Furthermore, it is only if they are able to expose populists and make decisions in a democratically proven manner that they will elect people who not only pursue their own interests but the interests of everyone.[3] There are those who believe that a government made of well-educated technocrats can achieve better results than an elected government. This may be true in theory; however, in practice, it is unlikely that such an altruistic government could exist and still satisfy people's need to live in a self-determined democracy. After all, democracy is a part of freedom and self-determination contributes to contentment.

## 9.5   Free of Charge

Equal opportunity can only be guaranteed if a free education is made available to everyone (see Sect. 6.6). This requires government funding. In countries where only the children of wealthy parents receive a good education because only the rich can afford it (in some cases even in the USA), equal opportunity is not possible.

---

[3]Some reprehensible dictators were initially elected by people who were not used to democracy, for example, Hitler and Mussolini. However, Erdogan in Turkey was also elected despite having had thousands of people arrested, disregarding the separation of powers, and waging wars—i.e. behaving like a dictator.

# Chapter 10
# Strategic Development of the European Union

## 10.1 Large Market

Distance is no longer an obstacle to world trade and as a result it is increasing rapidly. The quality and price of products and services are compared on a global scale and must therefore be competitive. However, bureaucratic hurdles continue to stand in the way of competitiveness and should be reduced if at all possible. At the very least they should be similar across the globe so that one provider is not favored over another. This applies to custom duties, licensing regulations, rules for competition, etc. Prosperity in a region is best served if its products can be sold all over the world without the constraints of extraneous regulations—i.e. only price and quality should be compared.[1]

The easiest thing to do is to create a single large market, which is what Europe did. Whoever works there can deliver throughout the market, free from bureaucratic restrictions. Those who do not belong to this market have to fill out customs forms and obtain approval for their products both in their own country and in the countries to which they deliver, etc. As a result, these products are correspondingly more expensive and less competitive.

Wherever there is a large open market, there must be uniform market rules and, of course, these must be accepted by all market participants. Whereas previously there were two or three political levels (municipal, state/regional, national) that had the authority to independently regulate numerous issues, there is now an additional political level, which is above the nation state and creates the rules for the large market.

---

[1]Anyone who introduces customs duties to protect their own economy (President Trump in the USA) has failed to recognize that they are making products more expensive and their own consumers pay the price. Consumers pay when they continue buying the foreign product or when local businesses make their similar product more expensive so as to be competitive with the foreign product.

© The Author(s) 2020

M. Meyer, *Liberal Democracy*, SpringerBriefs in Political Science,

https://doi.org/10.1007/978-3-030-47408-9_10

The supranational level must also negotiate rules governing economic relations with other markets (Europe/USA/China). It carries more weight than each individual country and contributes to the international standardization of regulations, which is in everyone's interest. Numerous different trade agreements such as are still in force today weaken the regulations, create confusion, and worsen the competitiveness of those who have to consider domestic political situations (e.g. agriculture) when negotiating trade agreements at the expense of others who can negotiate freely.

## 10.2   Peace Project

The European Union does not limit itself to the rules of the free market. It is not just an economic union; it is also a peace project that was created to prevent the catastrophe of war within its territory. And that is why the roots of the union run deep and additional regions are included. As a citizen of a country which is not part of the union, I can observe the union from the outside. And I have a positive feeling about the European Union and think it has achieved a great deal. However, there is one aspect of it that I will allow myself to criticize. I do not recognize a strategy that identifies which tasks should be dealt with on the supranational level and which should not. Rules concerning the assumption of tasks are missing—rules that would make the Union more successful.

## 10.3   Exclusive Responsibilities of the EU

The following areas should be under the sole jurisdiction of the EU:

- the Customs Union
- the rules of competition for the domestic market
- the monetary policy for Member States whose currency is the euro
- the conservation of marine biological resources under a common fisheries policy.
- common trade policies
- the establishment of international agreements.

Moreover, there are numerous tasks involving shared responsibility between the EU and member nations or with coordinating or supporting responsibilities of the EU. These additional responsibilities were assumed through numerous contracts between EU countries as the topic arose. From an outsider's perspective, these tasks were assumed without a plan or a concept. As a result, the EU is also involved in certain aspects of social policy, in agriculture and fisheries, in environmental policy, in consumer protection, in transport regarding trans-European networks, in energy, in security and in the area of law, in public health, in research, technological development and space, and in the areas of developmental cooperation and humanitarian aid. The EU also adopts measures to coordinate labor policy and it can take measures to coordinate social policies with regard to a common foreign and security policy.

This list is not exhaustive. However, it does give the impression that the EU is involved in numerous activities without a strategic goal. In the following pages I will outline the principles that should be taken into consideration when assuming new tasks.

## 10.4 Subsidiarity Principle

Although the subsidiarity principle is mandatory in the EU,[2] is it consistently observed?

Whenever possible, responsibilities and tasks belong at the lowest possible political level. People feel good if they can make decisions at a local level based on their peculiarities and needs. As a result, they are not "ruled from above". Countries with decentralized governments give their citizens a sense of having a direct say in issues that are most important to them. After all, it is most often local issues that are discussed by people, and which should, therefore, be decided locally.

Some European countries have a centralized government. This is because at one time in their history, an autocratic prince seized power (for example, in France, the Sun King, Louis IV, summoned regional princes to Versailles to keep them under his control). These princes were more concerned with maintaining their own centralized power than with working toward the good of the people. As a result, even today, decisions for all of France are made in Paris. For example, a permit to build a large building in the French territory just outside of Geneva, Switzerland would be granted from Paris rather than by the local authorities. However, a few hundred meters across the border in Switzerland, such a permit would be granted to the community by Canton Geneva. Italy is another example of centralized government. Permits to build new streets come from Rome, and it often takes months to receive an answer. A centralized system lacks efficiency and is too far removed from the people affected.

Is it really the case that all of the areas listed above as belonging to the jurisdiction of the EU can only be dealt with by the EU? And does the EU consistently reject tasks that should be dealt with at a lower political level?

When classifying tasks, the EU must consider the subsidiarity principle first. In so doing it would be placing the well-being of its citizens in all regions first. This would alleviate problems such as those in the Catalans, the Basque region, and in South Tyrol (which has meanwhile been resolved), as well as in many other regions.

---

[2]Art. 5 §. 3 TEU states: In areas of non-exclusive competence, the EU may act only "if and insofar as the objectives of the proposed action cannot be sufficiently achieved by the Member States, either at a central level or at a regional and local level, but can rather, by reason of the scale or effects of the proposed action, be better achieved at Union level."

## 10.5   Competition Between the Systems

A good economic environment helps to maintain overall competitiveness. The environment is established by policies, whereby the principle of subsidiarity means that numerous autonomous municipalities, regions, and states compete for the tasks that fall within their jurisdiction.

The principle of subsidiarity leads to competition among political units, in other words: competition between systems.

If every political responsibility is delegated as far down the line as possible, and each political unit decides autonomously which solution is best for an issue, it is not just a matter of being citizen-focused; it also promotes competition between political units. They compare their bureaucracies and adopt good practices from others. As a result, with time, the best solution to a problem prevails, which leads to a culture based on optimized solutions.

Even different tax rates compete with each other; they ensure that overall tax rates do not grow excessively.[3] Competition between different sets of building regulations, different employment conditions, and different health care costs ensure that the best solution stands out and prevails.

*Competition between systems* promotes the development of administratively optimal solutions and thus prosperity.

On an international level, competition between systems led to the downfall of communism in Eastern Europe. It was defeated by the free market economy of the West. It can be assumed that despite censorship and disinformation, modern communication methods, which mercilessly reveal the successes or failures of society, will prevent the permanent restriction of freedoms by dictators. Competition between systems will keep this from happening.

This conflict often plays out between those who are hardworking and those who are more easygoing. The former are in favor of competition in a free market society, while the latter strive to exclude competition. The former are decentralists and support the principle of subsidiarity (federalists), while the latter are centralists and support unified solutions (cartelists). Centralists must use force when implementing their statist solutions because these solutions also limit freedoms. However, society sets limits on coercion. The methods used during the inquisition of the Middle Ages or the gulag from the communist era are no longer tolerated. Criminal law prevents them. Therefore, there will always be groups that reject and avoid centralized solutions. The convenience of preventing competition will never last in a democratic society. At some point, the success seen in the better system will cause the other systems to restructure.

The principle of subsidiarity and the decentralization of power are one of the mainstays of prosperity. We must therefore resolutely oppose harmonization. The highest political level must not be increasingly given more responsibility.

---

[3]Tax cartels wish to harmonize taxes. They do not want tax competition but prefer to follow the European high-tax cartel in order to obtain additional revenue for redistribution.

In addition, it is important to focus on the overall picture rather than getting lost in details. It is impossible to establish absolute fairness with laws. Moreover, state intervention in the interest of small groups requires administration and increases bureaucracy. The government ratio rises. Those workers who generate the gross national product decrease in proportion to those who work as unproductive administrators. This too contributes to a reduction in prosperity.

Social groups that apply political pressure to gain privileges for themselves will one day realize that such advantages are not guaranteed to last. Even if government intervention initially helps achieve these goals, the wheel of history will continue to turn. Every plan becomes outdated. And when this happens, a new cascade of intervention begins to flow. Some will call for further measures to ensure the privileges they have gained. Others will once again try to undermine regulations by coming up with new ideas to get a piece of the pie. This in turn leads to calls for even stricter laws. In many cases only rigorous and disproportionate methods such as criminalization will help. Criminal law becomes a tool to safeguard special interests.[4] This downward spiral led to the police state among communists.

## 10.6  Excessive Bureaucracy

As the European Union incorporates concepts and seemingly acquires random new responsibilities, we might get the impression that its centralized bureaucracy is overflowing. If the correct "degree of curvature" for bananas is decreed by bureaucrats working from the centralized headquarters, then something has gone wrong with the allocation of responsibilities. Unfortunately, bureaucracy in Brussels leaves the impression that it is far too large and lacks democratic controls. As a result, many people are suspicious of the EU.

## 10.7  Core Responsibilities Have Not Been Delegated

In addition to organizing the economic market in Europe, the core responsibilities which belong to the supranational level include *foreign policy* and *security policy* (external *defense* and internal border control as well as the coordination of police investigations; on the other hand, police in general are a local responsibility). However, it is precisely these tasks that Europe finds difficult to delegate to the

---

[4]Almost every new law contains a paragraph on criminal offences. Apparently civil liability is no longer adequate to enforce legal obligations. In various countries the following are punishable: the violation of import quotas to protect agriculture; violation of information responsibilities towards customers in the financial service sector; failure to record company working hours—which in the era of the home office is especially absurd; violation of renter protection measures, etc.

supranational authorities. Politicians from the nation states still have much too great a claim to power.

## 10.8   Currency

A central currency strengthens the economic area and is preferable to many different national currencies. It is necessary to ensure that the region is not affected by the strong currencies of other larger economic areas and that it is not susceptible to blackmail by them.

However, this does not mean that debts should also be centralized (socialized). The task of the central bank is to ensure a stable currency. If municipalities, regional governments, or nations want to incur debts in the common currency, they should be allowed to do so. However, they should have to look for creditors who will give them loans, and they must negotiate the terms of these loans themselves. If they are in a strong financial position, they will receive a low interest rate on the money. If, however, there is a financial risk involved, they will either not receive money or will only be able to secure it at a high rate of interest. Should a creditor suffer a loss, the government borrowing the money must bear the burden on its own. There is no legal basis for a joint obligation with the other members of the community.

While it is true that joint and several liability for euro debts has not (yet) been introduced, southern Europeans are pushing this issue forward. When the sovereign debt in Greece was being restructured, the impression was given that joint and several liability already existed. At the time, the debt had to be restructured primarily because many European investors (pension funds, banks, etc. from France and Germany) had bought Greek government bonds without checking the creditworthiness of the borrower. This would have resulted in enormous financial difficulties for the creditors had Greece become insolvent. In effect, the socialization of debt was introduced through the back door to save these creditors. Rather than relying on the de facto joint and several liability of Europeans, it would be justified to require anyone buying government bonds to check the creditworthiness of the debtors, and then to bear any losses themselves.

I will now present both a negative and a positive example:

Italy has a massively oversized government, which devours around 60% of its GDP. This government is expensive and despite excessively high taxes, the private sector can barely bear the costs. When the country had its own currency (the lira), the government was financed by the Italian Central Bank, which issued new money each year. This led to a high rate of inflation. The value of money saved in the bank decreased annually. Those with savings accounts were financing the oversized government. With the introduction of the euro it was no longer possible to issue more money. However, interest rates in the Eurozone were so low that it was possible to finance the government by incurring more debt. It was only when the debts had become much too high that this was no longer possible. The heavily indebted Italian government, with a debt of roughly 135% of GDP,[5] is now demanding permission to incur additional debt, which is in breach of EU regulations. Borrowing money is easier than actually restructuring the government. After all, with a view to reelection it is better to make demands on Europe than it is to clean house.

Today, the European Central Bank supports member states by issuing new money and buying an unbelievable number of billions of euros worth of government bonds (from Italy?) each month so that national budgets can be financed. *Europe should not be financing countries with oversized and inefficient budgets with government bonds, thereby discouraging necessary restructuring. Rather it should encourage restructuring by requiring creditors to take responsibility for checking the creditworthiness of states.* The election of an Italian as head of the ECB did indeed lead to the rescue of such states by means of a zero or negative interest rate policy. Even a low interest rate would have had unacceptable consequences for overly indebted countries. Italy would have shared a fate similar to that of Argentina, a country that has repeatedly become insolvent in recent decades. Moreover, by putting this unbelievable number of billions of euros worth of government bonds on the market after they had been purchased, the ECB has promoted the de facto socialization of debt, in that customers who bought government bonds from them must now be protected.

The European states that are financially well-structured are being bled dry because of this policy. Saving is no longer worth their while. Their pension schemes, funds, etc. are suffering enormously. Why don't these countries defend themselves more vigorously?

The next example comes from my home country. When a municipality in the Canton of Valais (Leukerbad) could no longer pay its debts and became insolvent, both the Canton and the Confederation refused to help reduce the burden of debt. Even liability claims by a creditor stating that the canton had neglected its supervisory duties were rejected by the courts. The municipality was placed under supervision and had to undergo major restructuring and raise taxes. The municipality's creditors (funds, private pension funds, and private individuals) bore the losses themselves. As a result, investors now check the creditworthiness of communities and demand interest rates reflecting the amount of risk involved. Neither the Swiss government nor Swiss currency suffered any damage due to Leukerbad's insolvency.

It is not the ECB's job to finance the governments of member states. Its main responsibility is to ensure a stable currency. This does not include issuing billions to

---

[5]Italian debt: 134.8% of GDP (2018). Source: Statista Countries—‹Italy› National Debt of Italy until 2018. https://de.statista.com/statistik/daten/studie/167737/umfrage/staatsverschuldung-von-italien/

buy government bonds as this only discourages the long overdue restructuring of these states.[6]

## 10.9  External Impressions

Europe is the strongest economic region on earth. However, this region does not live up to its political strength. Therefore, in summary, I would like to make the following points about Europe:

- The European Union does not pay sufficient attention to the principle requiring responsibility be given to the lowest possible political level (the principle of subsidiarity). This applies to all issues—including the levying of taxes or the assumption of debt;
- All too often, the highest level of government intervenes, creating an oversized bureaucracy;
- This gives the impression of "government from above" with little democratic legitimacy;
- However, important responsibilities that should have been assigned to the highest level of government (defense, foreign policy) because the lower levels of government are not able to carry them out have not been assigned to this level. Nations continue to cling to their power in this area. Only trade policy with the associated areas (customs, competition policy, etc.) has been objectively assigned to the European level.

This leaves the impression that there is no coherent strategy to develop the European Union.

---

[6]It is also not the OECD's job to support the high-tax policies of such indebted states under the pretext of tax justice. Rather it should encourage the restructuring of such states to ensure that their locations become competitive when compared internationally (see Sect. 6.8).

# Chapter 11
# Good Governance

The principles of a prosperous state are summarized under the term "good governance". These include:

## 11.1 Corruption

Corruption is one of the enemies of constitutional states. It directs money into the hands of those who contribute nothing to prosperity. It does not reward achievement, but rather the illicit exercise of power. Entrepreneurs who have to give the Mafia part of their profits become frustrated. They wonder why they have to work while others earn money by doing nothing. Anyone in a powerful position in the government who receives private money in return for a permit is diverting funds into the pockets of those who have done nothing to earn it. They frustrate those who work and even prevent them from working in their chosen professions, hindering the success of those who labor. Those who collect such funds privately prevent its use for progress. Public servants should be selected according to their aptitudes and abilities (meritocracy) and not because of who they know.

Corruption of any kind lowers productivity and thus prosperity.[1]

Developing countries that observe the rules of good governance achieve success faster than corrupt countries. There are those who argue that countries that do not practice good governance should not be supported, because aid money flows into the wrong pockets, seeping away without bringing successful results.

---

[1]Redistribution by the government sometimes has the same effect as corruption. The state allocates funds to unproductive sectors of the economy or social classes, frustrating those who have had to work for their money. As a result, they enjoy their jobs less and their work begins to suffer. Such redistribution can be described as a "state of corruption".

© The Author(s) 2020
M. Meyer, *Liberal Democracy*, SpringerBriefs in Political Science,
https://doi.org/10.1007/978-3-030-47408-9_11

## 11.2   Constitutional State with Separation of Powers

The structure of the state with separate legislative, executive and judicial branches is a key element for success, whereby each branch must work *independently and efficiently*. Where one branch is above the other, the latter is no longer independent but carries out the wishes of the other power. This is the case when an autocrat subordinates either the parliament (legislative branch) or the judiciary branch or both. In such states, the legislative branch and/or the judicial branch do not function freely and independently. Both elements are a prerequisite for a thriving economy. In regions where the judicial branch is controlled by autocrats, the economy becomes wary of arbitrariness. It cannot develop freely, and foreign investment is discouraged. However, it is not enough for the judicial branch to be independent. It must also function efficiently so that the economy can rely on neutral rulings within a reasonable amount of time.

If a legal process takes too long, those concerned will begin asking themselves whether or not they want to call on the legal system at all—even if by doing so, they would receive justice. Anyone who has to wait too long for justice to be served begins looking for different types of solutions. As a result, people begin to avoid fulfilling contractual obligations because, after all, the other party cannot do anything about it anyway. White-collar criminals benefit because it is not worth the effort to prosecute. Except in genuinely complex cases, court proceedings should not take longer than a couple of months. This is quite possible as the courts in central and northern Europe have shown. On the other hand, Italy is an example of a country with an independent but inefficient judiciary. Court proceedings last for about 1 year. As a result, those seeking justice are denied their rights and often give up activities that are dependent on the law.

The *rule of law* and in particular *judicial independence* are essential for economic success. The former president of the European Court of Human Rights experienced a rather alarming example of an attempt to interfere with the courts. After retiring because of his age, he granted the *Neue Zurcher Zeitung* an interview (issue from 16 April, 2019 pages 13/15) Extracts from this interview are reproduced here (only his statements regarding Russia). The questions are shown in bold italics.

... I am particularly critical about how Russia has been dealt with.

*Why?*

In hindsight, I believe that Russia should not (yet) have been admitted into the Council of Europe in 1996. Significantly, this was also the conclusion reached at the time by the Council of Europe Commission, which carried out the relevant enquiries. Russia was simply not ready, and this was known. From the very beginning there were difficulties. Russia interfered in the smallest of matters, they even intervened in secretarial appointments at the highest level. They made it clear that they did not respect the independence of the Court of Justice. One day the Russian ambassador came to my office and on behalf of Putin demanded that I instruct the judges of the European Court of Human Rights (ECHR) as to how they were to decide in a particular case. Of course, I refused to do so in no uncertain terms. I made it clear to him, that this was an absolutely unacceptable violation of the independence of the courts.

*What were the results?*

The ambassador warned me that he would write a report about his visit and send it to Moscow. His face was quite red, and he left my office without saying goodbye. It was to be understood as nothing less than an open threat.

*And how did you react?*

First of all, I discussed the situation with my family. Was the situation too dangerous for us? My children were already adults at that time, so they gave me the freedom to decide for myself. I felt we could deal with the risk. Had my family reacted differently, I might have resigned as President of the Court. One thing was clear: Giving in to Russia's demands was out of the question. And I made that clear to Russia.

*Did Russia make good on its threat?*

A few days after the ambassador's visit, Russian state television broadcast a report claiming that the (ECHR) and I had been aware of the plans for a Chechen terrorist attack in Moscow but had kept it under wraps. It was a blatant attack on the credibility of the Court and on my integrity.

*And how did the Court react?*

I made it absolutely clear that the ECHR does not tolerate such methods. The EU backed the Court and me in a strongly worded statement, which calmed the situation on the surface. However, a Russian representative later warned me that my 'disobedience' to Putin had escalated the situation and I was the guilty party. This incident shows how Russia deals with the separation of powers. I have little doubt that Russian judges would be treated in the same manner as I had been.

*Shortly afterwards you became ill—and this was linked to the incident.*

During a trip to Russia in 2006, I suffered a life-threatening staphylococcal poisoning. The cause is unknown. The possibility that a third party administered the bacteria to me can, therefore, not be entirely eliminated. I have no proof, and I am not claiming that this is true. But it cannot be completely ruled out. At the time, I considered involving the legal authorities. However, I doubt that that would have been successful.

## 11.3 Respect for Civil Liberties

Respect for freedom of expression and its related human rights is essential for states that wish to rise to the top. These rights have freed the European spirit from autocratic bondage and are the basis for economic prosperity. In the meantime, human rights have been refined and supplemented with important additional fundamental rights. Civil liberties are not enough to ensure prosperity. Prosperity requires the *right to own property*. A free market economy presupposes the ownership of goods, the means of production, land and capital. Where property is vulnerable or poorly protected, prosperity is not possible.

*Freedom of the press* is one of the fundamental civil liberties. Wherever it is suppressed or even censored, there is no freedom of opinion and a true democracy is not possible.

## 11.4   Democracy

Is democracy a pre-requisite for economic success? With regard to China, some claim that democracy is not necessary. I addressed this question earlier (Sects. 2.3 and 2.4) and pointed out that without democratic freedom, the last stage of innovation necessary to reach the very top is missing.

Democracy is rule by the people. This rule can be exercised to different degrees. People's influence can be limited to legislative elections every few years, with this legislature then carrying out all other elections (in particular, the election of the government) and making all decisions. It can also give the people further responsibilities, such as electing a president or judges and finally it can assign decision-making powers to the people either compulsorily or by referendums.

Economic success is not dependent on the extent of the people's power. What is decisive, however, is that these responsibilities become so firmly rooted in the people's conscious that they remain sacred. A change of power by popular vote is a matter of course. Should an American president turn out to be an autocrat, the 22nd amendment to the constitution, which was ratified in 1951, prevents him/her from remaining in office for life. Democracy is so firmly anchored in the USA that a president must leave office after two terms. Elsewhere, if it is possible for a dictator to seize the power of the legislature so that parliament becomes irrelevant, or if they can overrule the judicial branch, Good Governance no longer exists, and economic success will begin to erode.

Democracy plays an important role in people's perception of their own freedom and happiness. They are more successful for this reason alone.

The subsidiarity principle, with its decentralization of responsibilities, is ultimately only possible within a democracy. It gives people the feeling that they are able to decide for themselves in their own regions and therefore they become competent and responsible citizens, who are satisfied with the system. Additionally, it promotes competition between the regions and leads to the best solutions for problems. Autocrats, on the other hand, want to exercise their authority, i.e. to centralize it, which limits success for the region.

Because autocrats are power driven, they strive for influence in other areas as well. For example, they want to expand their territory and annex other regions and they are sometimes willing to wage war in order to stay in power. They justify their aggressive foreign policy stance to their people and use it to enhance their reputations. Democracies, on the other hand, concentrate on themselves. They rarely try to exert any political influence on other countries and only go to war if they are forced to do so by autocratic aggressors.

A democracy that at the very least guarantees good governance within a country is a prerequisite for economic success.

* * *

Development in the direction previously described does not mean that the world will be perfect. It only means that the world will be better.

# Chapter 12
# Theses and Conclusion

In conclusion, I will summarize these insights into several theses:

- We do not know mankind's destiny. However, we should not leave our future evolutionary developments to chance, as we have done so far, but discover it ourselves. Finding this path is the goal.
- Education and training are the most important foundations for prosperity.
- In Europe, human rights established a new system of values based on self-responsibility and freedom. These values are the beginning of widespread prosperity for all.
- In prosperity, meaningful modernization and growth are necessary to maintain competitiveness and the standard of living. Only those who welcome innovation and create a culture open to change will remain at the top.
- Those people who reject change and search for ways to create advantages outside the realms of competition want to regulate the market to their own advantage. However, each such market intervention leads to higher prices. The number of market interventions reflects the price level and thus the standard of living within an economy.
- Protecting a social group from change and competition by implementing market interventions is always done at the expense of the general public and ultimately at the expense of everyone's prosperity—even that of the group which is ostensibly being protected. This group should only consider itself to be temporarily protected. The ever-growing backlog of groups requiring renewal will have to catch up at a later date and at a higher price.
- Government intervention requires government authority to enforce it. Since every system that restricts people's freedom is eventually undermined, the protection of privilege requires additional government authority. This leads to a spiraling of government intervention, which will become more oppressive and freedom will become even more restricted.
- Market interventions as well as a high degree of regulatory density lead to a redistribution of the funds generated. They are shown in the government ratio.

M. Meyer, *Liberal Democracy*, SpringerBriefs in Political Science,
https://doi.org/10.1007/978-3-030-47408-9_12

The higher the government ratio, the more people will depend on the state; the more favorable the culture is for additional government intervention, the lower the standard of living will fall. It is therefore urgent that *an instrument that limits the government ratio* is found.

- The possibilities for change are limited by the degree of regulation within a society. Regulation slows change. Whether an economy can maintain its impetus for renewal and level of prosperity—or even increase it—is reflected in the density of regulations. The more regulations there are, the higher the price levels will rise and the more the level of prosperity will fall. Therefore, it is urgently necessary that *a mechanism be found which limits regulatory density and permit requirements.*

- Too much government, a high degree of regulation density along with an oversized government apparatus to control it, too many redistributions and a high government ratio all have to be paid for. Taxes go up. The middle-class finances it while its own level of prosperity erodes. It defends itself by expressing a lack of trust in established political parties, and then begins voting for marginal parties. Alternatively, it may even heed the call of an autocrat. Democracy comes under threat.

- Measures against this include: reducing demands made on the government, streamlining the government, and reducing the amount or redistribution as well as the government ratio; reducing taxes and duties, especially for the middle class and also for other taxpayers (no new redistributions).

- An ever-increasing government with tax increases to finance it and the use of tax harmonization to impose the higher taxes limit prosperity and ultimately endanger democracy.

* * *

*Liberal democracy* has brought unprecedented prosperity to many people. It is the only successful value system so far. With this book, I have aimed to outline the direction in which it should continue to develop. Hopefully, the inertia shown by affluent societies combined with dubious attacks by autocrats will not prevent this development.

A liberal economy is a prerequisite for a nation to reach the top.

Liberalism is not a political system. It is a set of economic rules. These rules foster competition within a fixed legal structure. Competition has led to innovations, research and tremendous productivity, i.e. it has greatly promoted progress with prosperity.

However, liberalism must be complemented by freedom and legal security with an independent judiciary, as well as equal opportunity. Laws must guarantee the rule of law. "Good Governance" is the prerequisite for success. This presupposes a stable democracy that cannot be decimated by autocrats who attempt to change the rules in their favor.

Autocrats claim that illiberalism (Russia and a few Eastern European countries) or dictatorships supported by technocrats (China and other Southeast Asian countries) are more efficient and lead to prosperity more quickly than liberalism based on a democratic constitutional foundation. More than anything else, such assertions serve to justify their own systems and their own power. It is true that the initial steps toward *prosperity* can perhaps be more efficiently realized with autocratic leadership that is actually interested in the wellbeing of the people and not simply in their own power. However, as soon as a certain level of prosperity has been reached, people demand *well-being*—in other words, they demand freedom and co-determination. Only in such an atmosphere do they drive development towards the top.

Countries with a tradition of human rights have a much better environment for the development of a good economy. They will always maintain their advantage over autocracies.

The rules of the game for liberalism are neither politically right nor left. Liberalism should not be pushed into the politically right arena, as is being increasingly done in Europe. Liberalism and the welfare state are not opposites. On the contrary, liberalism used to be regarded as politically left; it still is in the USA.

Attacks on liberal democracy come not only from autocrats, but also from within. For example, tremendous overregulation weakens entrepreneurs and an equally tremendous flood of laws with heavy redistribution leads to a burden on a middle class that can no longer bear it. A strong middle class is important for a peacefully prosperous society. Ultimately, life within a welfare state continually brings ideologies or even political parties to the surface that still dream of outdated economic systems (such as Marxism) which have up till now never been proven to work anywhere.

In politics, it is usually a question of whether "more or less government intervention" is needed. The core question is whether the state should favor continual renewal within liberal regulations or whether it should provide security within comfortable but rigid structures that could even be considered autocratic. Therein lies the economic tension between right and left in the political arena.

Only if this fundamental conflict is resolved in favor of those who prefer a free market system to a state controlled one can the economy continue to prosper in everyone's interest. Only then can liberalism continue to promote progress.

\* \* \*

# References

AEUV (2012) Treaty on the functioning of the European Union. Official Journal of the European Union (Eurolex). C 326/47. 26 October. Consolidated Version of the Treaty on the Functioning of the European Union—PROTOCOL—protocol (Nr. 2) on the application of the principles of subsidiarity and proportionality (Official Journal Nr. 115 from May 09, 2008, pp. 0206–0209)

Böckenförde E-W (2007) The secularized state. Its character, its justification and its problems in the 21st century. Themed Volume 86 of the Carl Friedrich von Siemens Foundation. Carl Friedrich von Siemens Stiftung, Munich. ISBN 978-3-938593-06-6

Dawkins R (2016) The selfish gene. Oxford University Press

Der Spiegel (2019) Forschungsgruppe für Weltanschauungen in Deutschland (Research Group for World Views in Germany), vol 17/2019 from 19 April 2019 cited among others by "fowid". www.fowid.de

Eurostat – EU-SILC (2015) Income disparities are narrowing. Neue Zürcher Zeitung, 4 August (or version from 28 March 2017)

Federal Statistical Office (2019a) Police Crime Statistics 2018. https://www.bfs.admin.ch/bfs/de/home/aktuell/neue-veroeffentlichungen.assetdetail.7726202.html. Accessed 2 Apr 2020

Federal Statistical Office (2019b) Structure of the permanent resident population by canton 1999–2018. https://www.bfs.admin.ch/bfs/de/home/statistiken/kataloge-datenbanken/tabellen.assetdetail.9466879.html. Accessed 3 Apr 2020

Federal Statistical Office (2020) Standard of living and inequality of income distribution in selected European countries. https://www.bfs.admin.ch/bfs/de/home.assetdetail.11467945.html. Accessed 2 Apr 2020

Federal Statistical Office (o.J.) Inequality of income distribution. https://www.bfs.admin.ch/bfs/de/home/statistiken/wirtschaftliche-soziale-situation-bevoelkerung/soziale-situation-wohlbefinden-und-armut/ungleichheit-der-einkommensverteilung.html. Accessed 2 Apr 2020

Hegel GWF (1817) Encyclopedia of the philosophical sciences in basic outline. Heidelberg

Hesse H (2008) Letter to Wilhelm Gundert (Sept. 1960). In: Lindenberg U (ed) My Hermann Hesse – a reader. Suhrkampsss

International Monetary Fund (IMF) (2020) World economic outlook, January 2020. https://www.imf.org/en/Publications/WEO/Issues/2020/01/20/weo-update-january2020. Accessed 3 Apr 2020

Khanna P (2019) The future is Asian. The Orion Publishing Group Ltd. (Weidenfeld & Nicolson), London

Landes D (1910) The wealth and poverty of nations: Why some are so rich and some so poor. W.W. Norton, New York

© The Author(s) 2020
M. Meyer, *Liberal Democracy*, SpringerBriefs in Political Science,
https://doi.org/10.1007/978-3-030-47408-9

Link A (2019) Unbelievable how many Germans believe in hell! Bild.de, 8 June. https://www.bild.
    de/politik/ausland/politik-ausland/umfrage-zu-pfingsten-glauben-die-deutschen-noch-an-
    himmel-und-hoelle-62449638.bild.html. Accessed 3 Apr 2020

Neue Zürcher Zeitung (2019) It was nothing short of an outright threat. Neue Zürcher Zeitung,
    16 April, pp 14–15

Olson M (1982) The rise and decline of nations. New Haven, London

Piketty T (2013) Capital in the 21st century publisher. C.H. Beck (original French title Le Capital au
    XXIe siècle published in August 2013)

Rosling H (2018) Factfulness. Ten reasons we're wrong about the world – and why things are better
    than you think. Flatirion Books, New York

Statista (2019a) Life expectancy of men and women in Germany at birth during the period from
    1871 to 2018. https://de.statista.com/statistik/daten/studie/185394/umfrage/entwicklung-der-
    lebenserwartung-nach-geschlecht/. Accessed 2 Apr 2020

Statista (2019b) Statistics on life expectancy. https://de.statista.com/themen/47/lebenserwartung/.
    Accessed 2 Apr 2020

Statista (2019c) Italy: Government debt from 1988 to 2018 and forecasts until 2024. https://de.
    statista.com/statistik/daten/studie/167737/umfrage/staatsverschuldung-von-italien/.    Accessed
    19 Mar 2020

UNICEF Report (2019) Child mortality worldwide: Why do children die?, 19 September. https://
    www.unicef.de/informieren/aktuelles/blog/kindersterblichkeit-weltweit-warum-sterben-kinder/
    199492. Accessed 13 Apr 2020

United Nations (2015) Resolution of the General Assembly. Adopted on 25 September 2015.
    https://www.un.org/Depts/german/gv-70/band1/ar70001.pdf. Accessed 13 Mar 2020

Printed in the United States
By Bookmasters